CHOTEAU
Creek

A Sioux Reminiscence

Joseph Iron Eye Dudley

UNIVERSITY OF NEBRASKA PRESS: LINCOLN & LONDON

⊗ The paper in this book meets the minimum require-
ments of American National
Standard for Information Sciences –
Permanence of Paper for Printed Library
Materials, ANSI Z39.48-1984.

First Bison Books printing: 1998
Most recent printing indicated by the last digit below:
10   9   8   7   6   5   4   3   2   1

Library of Congress Cataloging in Publication Data
Dudley, Joseph Iron Eye, 1940–
Choteau Creek: a Sioux reminiscence /
Joseph Iron Eye Dudley.   p. cm.
ISBN 0-8032-1690-4 (cl.: alkaline paper)
ISBN 0-8032-6611-1 (pa.: alkaline paper)
1. Dudley, Joseph Iron Eye, 1940–.
2. Yankton Indians – Biography.
3. Yankton Indians – Social life and
customs. I. Title. E99.Y25D833 1992
928.3'382–dc20 91-39285 CIP

TO THE MEMORY OF MY GRANDPARENTS

WILLIAM AND BESSIE BOURISSAU

AND TO ALL GRANDPARENTS WHO

PARENT THEIR GRANDCHILDREN

Preface

Turning the clock back in memory to write a book about two persons whose lives touched and influenced my life as none others have is one of the most difficult, and yet most rewarding, tasks I have ever undertaken. It required going back in thought and imagination to that little brown house tucked back into a basin on the rolling prairie of the Yankton Sioux Reservation. Choteau Creek, the eastern boundary of the reservation, ran no more than fifty yards from the house. Now it is nearly dry, but then it unfailingly provided physical sustenance.

The Yankton Reservation, in southeastern South Dakota, is one of nine federally recognized reservations in the state. Its southern boundary lies along the Missouri where that river begins to separate South Dakota from Nebraska. It encompasses approximately 660 square miles. The 1990 census lists the population as a little less than 2,000 American Indians and a substantially large number of non-Indians. Closer to the time of this story, the 1960 census shows the nonwhite population to have been about 1,460 persons.

Of course, when we speak of American Indians, we are speaking about poor people. On my reservation, approximately 51 percent of all household incomes fall below the poverty level, with a median household income of about $7,600 per year, compared with a national figure of $16,841 per year (1980 census). At the time of which I am writing, the discrepancy was even greater in relative terms.

Writing about the people back there meant recalling not only what poverty can do to a people, but what quality of character and faith can exist in the midst of it. I thought about persons whom I hadn't thought about in years—people who had once enriched my life and who enriched it again in the remembering. These were not persons involved in tribal government, political movements, and other activities that catch the eye of the media. Rather, they were the quiet, common American Indians who influenced people like myself by applying their beliefs in the examples they set throughout their day-to-day lives.

There are three traditional dialects spoken in the Sioux language: Dakota, Lakota, and Nakota. The dialect spoken by my grandmother and most of the people in this story is Dakota, which is the dialect or language of the Yankton Sioux. In a few places the translation is dependent upon the diction and tone of voice, and therefore it is difficult to make an exact translation. Sometimes, too, there is no English word equivalent to what is being said in Dakota.

For nearly twenty years, as I have shared bits and pieces of my story, I have been encouraged by countless persons to write this book. I never took any of them very seriously until I returned, after an absence of some twenty-four years, as the minister of two small churches not far from home. On the second Sunday I briefly talked about my grandparents, as part of my message. After the worship service I overheard one woman say to another, "This minister will do all right; I knew his grandparents." That was the unexpected "push" to begin writing this book.

This, then, is a story about my maternal grandparents, William and Bessie Bourissau, and my life with them. I have cautiously and deliberately worked to describe not ideal persons, but persons with all their flaws and imperfections, although in one sense they were saints: people whose lives and character were of such virtuous quality that I dared to recall them as whole persons. There was a time when I referred to their home, that little brown house where I was raised, as out in the middle of nowhere. Yet that is where I learned the social, cultural, and spiritual values that have stayed with me everywhere I have been. While Choteau Creek sustained our physical life, my grandparents sustained my spiritual life.

I want to express my appreciation to my wife, Avon, for her constant support and encouragement to continue working on the book, and for her critique and suggestions, which were invaluable. A word of thanks goes to all of those countless persons who kept the writing spark alive by their encouragement. You were an important part of this accomplishment.

For you, the reader, I hope this book will touch your life and warm your heart, not so much because of the way it is written, but because of who the story is about. I had good material from which to draw.

J.I.E.D.

I

Much of life seems to consist of change and turning points. That is probably why December of 1948 is so indelibly etched in my mind. At the time, one of my two brothers and my sister and I were living with our maternal grandparents on the Yankton Sioux Indian Reservation in southeastern South Dakota. Even though we visited our parents occasionally, we had actually lived with Grandpa and Grandma ever since Mom and Dad were divorced, about five years before. At one time all four of us kids lived with our grandparents in that little three-room house.

Phillip was the oldest. He was tall and thin, with a large-featured face. He had big ears about which everyone used to tease him. A very mischievous person with a good sense of humor, he was pigeon-toed and walked with an awkward gait that went along with his lighthearted personality. Like the rest of us, Phillip attended the red brick one-room school about two miles north of the house, but he and I never went to school together. Because he was seven years older than I, and because he had skipped a grade, he graduated from the eighth grade the year before I started.

When Phillip was thirteen years old, he left home and began earning his own living.

Dorothy was next to the oldest. She had just turned thirteen in 1948 and was in the seventh grade. Of the four of us, she had the lightest complexion. She was thin and of medium height, with long dark-brown hair. She was an assertive young woman with mood swings that went along with it. Perhaps her assertiveness developed as a result of having to hold her own among three brothers. Dorothy loved school and was good at it. On days when Grandpa thought the weather was too cold or stormy for us to walk to school, she would cry and pout most of the morning.

David, rather dark and on the chunky side, was two years older than I. Of all the kids, he and I spent the most time together when we were growing up. But he was different from the rest of us; he didn't like school at all. He stayed in the first grade two years, and when he was in the fourth grade he was put back into the third grade, so there came a time when he and I were in the same grade. Because we were so different, however, there was never any competitiveness between us. I was more an indoors person while he loved to be outside. He became an excellent hunter and provided lots of wild game for our table. He loved sports and often begged me to play catch with him. He was constantly climbing trees, it seemed, and his pants were always worn out on the seat or the knees. Grandma gave him the name "Onzoġe Yuḣdeca," which means "Torn Pants" in the Dakota language. Behind his dark-brown eyes and almost coal-black hair was a rather quiet person who seemed to be observing most of the time.

Mom lived in Sioux City, Iowa. Most of her life she worked in the packing house, or in a dry-cleaning establishment as a pants presser. After the divorce she developed an alcohol problem, which became a way of drowning out the hurt and rejection. She was of medium build, with long, black hair, rough complexion,

2

and a large nose. She, too, was rather assertive, and inherited her loud voice from Grandpa.

We hadn't heard from Mom for what seemed like a long time. She came home once a year or so but didn't stay very long, just a day or two. She wrote to Grandma and Grandpa only about twice a year. Early in the fall of 1948 the packing house near where she worked had an explosion, but we didn't know if she was one of the casualties. She didn't notify us, let us know that she wasn't injured. I'll never forget the fear that came over me as we sat listening to the names of the killed and injured being read over the radio, one by one. Or the feeling of relief as the announcer came to the end of the list without mentioning her name. Still we didn't hear from Mom for several months following this event.

Dad lived in Yankton, South Dakota, about sixty miles from us. He was full-blood Sioux and a member of the Yankton Tribe. A handsome man with a personality that attracted women, he was of medium height and had smooth, light-brown skin, dark-brown eyes beneath heavy brows, and black wavy hair that he combed straight back. He was a neat dresser and always wore a suit and tie. I had never seen him in jeans or overalls. He was probably one of the cleverest persons I knew—the salesman type—but he worked at many different kinds of jobs and did well at all of them. He was a very creative person and, given a little time, could figure out how to make or fix anything. He was a perfectionist and could prepare an excellent meal, decorate a Christmas tree beautifully, and make Christmas presents look like they were wrapped in the department store.

We heard from Dad only once in a while; being a father was not a very high priority in his life. Phillip lived near him, but they didn't see each other very often either. The last time we had heard from Dad was two years earlier. That was the year we three younger children went to Yankton to spend Christmas with him and his wife. As soon as we arrived, he gave us our largest

Christmas presents. He had bought new coats for all of us and, best of all, new sleds. Most of our vacation we played on the James River, which flowed by his house. At the end of the two weeks Dad took us back to Choteau Creek, to our grandparents.

It was always good to be with Dad; there was a feeling of warmth and excitement. Often he took time to play with us. When our visit was over, however, the parting was sad and tearful. Dorothy would start to cry first. Dad would try to hug all three of us at the same time, and with sadness on his face, he would promise to write and to come to see us real soon. But deep down we knew he wouldn't keep his promise and we wouldn't see or hear from him again for a long time. We would go back to school watching for the mail carrier to stop at our mailbox, which was near the school, and waiting for a letter from Dad, but it very seldom came.

Most of our association with other people our age took place during the school year. We lived too far from other families to spend much time with them. The closest family with children our age lived about two miles away. Only occasionally, during the summer months, would some kids walk down to our place for something to do. We'd usually go swimming in Choteau Creek. During the school year, however, we enjoyed playing and sharing other activities with our schoolmates.

Generally we were the only family that had to walk to school, especially during the winter. To get to the schoolhouse we followed the dirt road, just two tracks worn into the earth, around the edges of the fields and past the dam until we came to another dirt road that went straight north. Years before, the road that went north was part of the mail route. Then Grandma and Grandpa's mailbox was under a tall cottonwood tree only a quarter of a mile from their house. About a mile from the school the road went over a big hill. When we got to the top of it we could see for miles around. From there the school looked like a doll's

4

house. At the bottom of the hill the road turned into a gravel road that went by the school. In the wintertime, the cold north wind hit us full force from the time we reached the hilltop until we got to school. Sometimes we walked backward to keep from freezing our faces.

Our schoolhouse was one of the nicest, newest buildings in the county. It was of red brick and had a nice basement where we used to play when rain or snowstorms kept us inside. The upstairs had hardwood floors. Both the front and back (north and south) walls were covered by huge chalk boards. The west wall was all windows. On the east side of the room was the entrance with a place to hang our coats and leave our lunch pails, the library, and a door that led to a storage room where the telephone was. The desks were lined up in four rows across the room, sometimes facing the teacher and other times with our backs to her. The youngest children usually sat at the front. There were never more than a total of twenty-four students in the eight grades. Some grades would have as many as five or six pupils, while others would have only one. The teacher had two short benches beside her desk where she met with each class or combination of classes during each of the four periods during the day. About half the students were white and the other half were Indian. Most of the time we got along well.

At recess the games we played and the things we did went in cycles. One month playing on the merry-go-round was the thing to do. The next month we would play the game called "I'll draw the frying pan." In the winter, after a fresh snow, we played "fox and goose" or made snowmen or built forts. In the spring we played softball; then we all played on the swings. But always, everything seemed to go in cycles.

We had Halloween parties, Valentine parties, Easter parties, and the last celebration of the school year was the school picnic.

Those were times when everyone brought food and we ate until we were filled to the brim.

Christmas was the most exciting time of the year. We always had a Christmas program that took weeks of preparation. We practiced our singing and had to learn our pieces and parts for the plays. At least a month before the program we drew names to see who would give Christmas gifts to whom. About a week before the program we decorated the Christmas tree and the whole schoolroom. With each passing day, the closer we got to the night of the program, the less we studied and the more we practiced. The day before the program we built the stage, using the same planks that were stored away from the previous years. In front of the stage we hung long, black curtains on a heavy wire stretched across the room. Then we practiced the whole program, from start to finish, sliding the curtains open and shut as though all the parents and friends were out there.

The day of the program we stayed at school only half the day, long enough to set up more seats and practice one more time, then we went home to get ready for the night. About five o'clock in the evening we put on our best clothes, took the gifts for the exchange, and walked back to school. After the gifts were placed under the tree, all the students went back into the storeroom where the telephone was and waited for our turn in the program. We were supposed to remain very quiet back there, but with all the excitement that was hard to do.

Before the Rural Electrification Administration brought electricity to the school, the farmers used to bring gas lamps and lanterns that were hung from the schoolroom ceiling during the program. Even when Grandma was along in years, she walked to the school and sat among all the other parents who came to watch the Christmas program. After the program, we exchanged our gifts and Santa Claus would arrive, bringing everyone candy and peanuts, and a Christmas present for every student from the teacher.

6

Then there was the long, cold walk home in the moonlight. By the time the program was over, we looked forward to being home with Grandpa and Grandma and sharing the Christmas excitement with them.

For some reason this year was different. One bright, brisk morning in early December, while we were in school, the telephone began to ring. It was a ring that lasted forever. Five longs—that was the party-line ring for our school. Dad was calling to tell us he wanted us to come to his place and spend our Christmas vacation with him. I sat in school the rest of the day wrestling with a strange feeling inside me. It was good to hear Dad's voice again, but this year I didn't look forward to being with him during vacation.

The two-mile walk back home that evening was longer than ever because all while we walked David and Dorothy talked about how excited and eager they were to go to Dad's. They could hardly wait. How was I to tell them I didn't want to go with them? How could I make them understand? I really didn't know why I didn't want to go—it wasn't that I didn't love Dad any more—I only knew that I wanted to be with Grandpa and Grandma this Christmas.

As we neared the house, the excitement began to rise. "Wait till we tell Grandpa and Grandma the news!" When something exciting happened during the day we always raced to the house to tell the news, the one who got there first, of course, being the first to tell. Today there were only two running the race. My enthusiasm had been dimmed by that strange feeling which by now was saying, "Not only do I not want to go this year, but I am not supposed to go."

As the days moved on, it appeared to me that no one sensed the aloneness I felt in the midst of all the excitement. Why didn't anyone ask me if I was going to Dad's house? Nobody seemed to care. But what would I say even if they did ask? Plans were being made and it was assumed that I would be going, too. There came the dreadful thought that I might have to go even though I didn't want to—and wasn't supposed to.

One day the mail carrier brought a letter addressed to Dorothy. Whenever Dad wrote to the three of us, he always addressed the letter to her. After all, she was the oldest of us three, and being the only girl in our family, she was sort of Dad's favorite. I began to feel some relief because the letter was not addressed to me. Inside was enough money for three bus tickets. Dad also informed us that he had called our closest neighbor, Art Satler, and asked him to take us to the bus station on the specified day. Everyone knew we didn't have an automobile. Grandpa and Grandma had had a Model-T when they were young, but they never owned a car while we lived with them.

Two days before we were to leave, I was awakened early in the morning by Grandpa fixing the fire in the potbelly stove. Grandpa was a noisy person. Everytime he did something, he made lots of noise. When he talked, he did so in a loud voice. When he slept, he snored loudly. Even when he walked, he walked heavily—and he didn't seem to care who heard him or who he woke up.

Grandpa wasn't originally from the Yankton reservation. In fact, he wasn't even Sioux. He was half Chippewa and half French. When he was young, he had been a tall, straight man, but now he was old and stooped. His white wavy hair accentuated his blue eyes that sometimes glared with sternness and strength and other times sparkled with mischief.

Grandma was a full-blood Sioux, a member of the Yankton Tribe who had lived on the reservation all her life. She was a tiny, frail-looking woman with long hair that was pinned up in a roll across the front and a bun in the back of her head. Her soft voice seemed to match the frailness of her body. Yet she was a person who did things in a hurry and walked at a rapid pace. Her gentle, dark-brown eyes and the frown wrinkles on her forehead always reminded us of her kindness and how seriously she took most of life. When she looked down at the floor, or covered her eyes with her hand, and began to speak, everyone listened, for we knew that what she said was worth hearing and remembering.

After Grandpa finished starting the fire that morning, he returned to their bed, which was not far from where David and I slept. He and Grandma began to talk, as they often did in the middle of the night or early in the morning before anyone else was awake. It didn't take long before their conversation focused on our planned Christmas vacation away from them. It was evident that this was foremost in both their minds.

There were a few moments of conversation when, suddenly, I could not believe what I was hearing! Grandpa was saying to Grandma, "Joseph doesn't want to go with the other two." That was all he said, and Grandma never questioned him. How did he know? It was a mystery to me. I didn't remember saying anything to anyone about not wanting to go. In all the excitement he apparently was very much aware of my aloneness.

The next morning while we were eating breakfast, Grandpa broke the news to David and Dorothy. He told them in such a diplomatic manner that nobody questioned him and no one was hurt or angry. There were times when Grandpa said a lot of things in order to say a little of something very important. This time he didn't say that I told him I didn't want to go, nor did he say that he didn't want me to go. He only said I would not be going.

Two days later, on a Saturday morning, David and Dorothy were off on a two-week vacation with our father. The day of their departure was unusually warm. Grandma had decided to go along to the bus station to see them off. She rolled her long, gray hair that morning and got out her good shoes. As she dressed, she put on her best pair of cotton stockings. When they were ready to leave, Grandma bundled up like she was going to the North Pole. Being only eight years old, I didn't think it was necessary for her to bundle up like that; after all, the weather was so pleasant. But that's the way Grandma was. Her little frail body couldn't stand too much wind and cold, so she always prepared for the worst possible weather. They would have to walk about a mile, through the woods and across Choteau Creek, to the neighbor's house.

I too dressed warmly and walked with them as far as the creek. A knot came to my throat when I said good-bye to David. The tightness there was almost too much for me as I hugged Dorothy, said good-bye, and through tear-filled eyes wished her a merry Christmas. I watched from the bank as they made their way across the creek on the ice and up the bank, following the foot-prints that had been made in the snow by others who had come that way.

Had I made the right decision, not to go? When they came home full of stories about their vacation, would I be sorry I hadn't gone with them? Almost immediately I felt a nearly unbearable emptiness. For a brief moment I wanted to call out and ask them to wait for me, but there wasn't enough time for that. I just stood there with tears streaming down my cheeks, wondering. By then they were across the creek and over the bank on the other side. Before they disappeared from sight, David turned and, without stopping, waved at me. Then Dorothy stopped, turned, and paused for a moment and, with a forced smile on her face, waved one last good-bye.

Grandma never said a word, nor did she look back even once. She just continued to walk at a steady pace, constantly looking down at the snow as though she was carrying a heavy burden that was almost too much for her. Then all three of them were gone, out of sight.

Little did we know that Dad never intended to send us kids

back to Grandpa and Grandma at the end of the Christmas vacation. He knew that if Grandpa was aware of this, he wouldn't allow us to go. David would come back a few months later, but Dorothy never returned home again to live.

I sat on a tree stump for a few moments, listening. There was a stillness in the air, broken only by the raucous calling of a crow in the far distance and the trickling sound coming from the shallow part of the creek, water flowing over and around the rocks.

2

The walk back to the house seemed awfully long. The glare from the sun shining down on the snow was extra bright that day. Most of the snow had melted off the roof of the house. The weather was so sunny and warm it tempted one to think winter would be very short that year (but people in that part of the country know better than to think such thoughts in the middle of December).

I sat on the porch for a few minutes, trying to regain my composure. Around the corner came our little brown-haired terrier. Sitting beside me, he looked the other direction as though he didn't want to embarrass me by watching my struggle to hold back the tears. Finally, when he apparently felt I had pulled myself back together, he pushed his nose between my arm and my waist until his head rested on my lap. We sat there, just the two of us, listening to the water from the melting snow drip off the edge of the roof and watching each drip make an imprint in the snow on the ground below.

Grandpa would wonder what had happened to me if I didn't go into the house soon. But that was all right; I had made the adjustment—accepted the immediate results of my decision not to go—and now I was ready to let Grandpa know I was back.

Getting up from the porch, I entered the "old kitchen." I never understood why we referred to it by that name. This room wasn't any older than the rest of the house, but it was in worse condition than the other two rooms. We lived in the "old kitchen" only during the summer months. In the winter it was always cold, and very dark because the window on the north side was covered with an old door that Grandpa had made to keep out the north wind. Grandma's round flour bin occupied the far corner. In the middle of the north wall, in front of the darkened window, stood an old table with a few empty glass jars on it, along with an empty salt shaker and an old spoon. In a second corner was the cupboard used to store the extra dishes and bowls that weren't used very often. In the third corner, and covering about one-fourth of the room, was a large pile of wood that Grandpa had split. It was stacked against an old trunk, turned lengthways to keep the woodpile neat. Finally, in the corner next to the door, hung some old winter coats that hadn't been worn for quite some time. Most of them belonged to Grandpa. Since he was no longer able to work and hunt and do the things he used to do when he was younger, most of his winter coats just hung there, winter after winter.

Opening the door that led to the rest of the house, I pushed by the quilt that hung over the doorway to help keep out the cold. Just inside was the cookstove, which extended out into the middle of the room. To the very right, somewhat behind the stove and near the reservoir, was the washstand with the basin sitting on it. The reservoir was connected to the end of the stove and held water, making it convenient to dip out warm water to wash with on cold winter days. The cupboard that held all the everyday dishes and most of the staple foods stood to the left. In the middle of the room was the table, covered with a red checkered oilcloth and flanked by two straight-backed chairs. Immediately beyond the table was the folding bed where David and I slept when the three of us kids were there.

The third room was always referred to as "the other room." It was connected to the winter kitchen by a wide doorway. To the immediate right was the old potbelly stove that was set up in the fall and taken down and stored in the "old kitchen" in the spring. On the wall to the left hung Grandpa and Grandma's better coats and dresses. Next there was Grandpa's pack-battery radio sitting on an old washstand. Between the clothes on the wall and the radio was the east door, which was sealed shut with old rags stuffed around the edges in the winter. It was opened for ventilation in the summer but was never used as an entrance and exit because the screen door was always nailed shut. The room also contained Grandpa and Grandma's bed with the iron bedstead, Grandma's sewing machine, the dresser with its big oval mirror, and the three-quarters bed where Dorothy slept and where I would sleep while David and Dorothy were gone.

As I entered the winter kitchen, Grandpa was sitting in his wicker rocking chair beside the cookstove. He looked up at me and asked in his firm yet kind manner, "Is my boy all right?" Choking back the tears, trying to relax the muscles around my mouth, I replied, "Yah, Grandpa, I'm all right." But I wasn't all right and he knew it. Reaching out toward me, he said, "Come here." That was almost more than I could stand. He took me on his lap, and I cried until it seemed as though I had no more tears. I could feel his rough whiskers against my face as he tried to comfort me.

Yes, Grandpa always seemed to have the time and to know what to say when someone was hurting deep inside. At times he was a very harsh man who ruled our home with an iron hand. At times he was not very patient with me or anyone else, but one always knew where one stood with him, because he was a plain and outspoken person. Yet at other times, like this, he was very patient, kind, and understanding. When he said he knew how I was feeling it was more than just rhetoric. It was quite clear that he did know and he cared.

I sat on his lap and cried until I could cry no more. Between my sobs, he assured me that we would have a good Christmas, that he and Grandma were glad that I would be with them that year. When I began to calm down he suggested that I lie down and take a nap. That certainly was an unusual suggestion coming from him, a man who lived by the dictum "early to bed, early to rise" and believed there was no time for naps during the day.

Grandpa reached into his pocket, pulled out a big red handkerchief, and dried my tears. Then he held the handkerchief over my nose and said, "Now blow." He gently wiped my nose. I could see in front of my face his big, strong, gentle hand with the little finger missing. Getting up from his lap, I went into the "other room" and lay down on the bed in the corner, Dorothy's bed. I lay there recalling the events of the past few weeks and couldn't help but wonder what they would lead to. With that, I fell asleep.

In what seemed like only seconds later, I woke to the sound of whispering voices in the kitchen; Grandma and Grandpa were talking to each other. I must have slept for several hours, and so soundly that I didn't even hear Grandma come home.

It was a wise decision for Grandma to bundle up the way she had. Before she arrived home, the sun went behind the clouds, the wind began to blow, and the temperature dropped below the freezing mark. I heard Grandpa say he was going to bring in some more wood before it was covered with snow. Then he added, "Shall I bring it in when I am finished?" I didn't hear a reply, but there must have been one—the nodding of a head—because he left immediately without saying another word.

Grandma came into the room where I was lying still half asleep. I suppose that in earlier days she would have just peeked into the room to see if I was awake, but cataracts had clouded her eyes now and she had to walk to my bedside before she could tell. She asked her usual question, "Are you asleep?" Sometimes, just to tease her, I would answer, "Yes," and pretend that I was snoring. This, however, was no day for teasing.

"Are you asleep?" she asked. "No." I replied. "Would you like an apple and some peanuts?" she went on. "Yes." That was really only a half truth. I did want an apple, but I never really cared for peanuts in the shell. Both Grandma and Grandpa, however, enjoyed sitting down together, shelling and eating roasted peanuts while they visited. So every Christmas they bought a large sack of peanuts in the shell.

She handed me a little brown paper sack. Inside were a few pieces of hard candy, along with perhaps two big handfuls of roasted peanuts in the shell. Then she gave to me a large red Delicious apple. I could feel myself beginning to cheer up, although I'm sure it wasn't because of the peanuts. Maybe the apple had something to do with it, but it was mostly because Grandpa and Grandma understood how I felt, and because I knew they were happy they would not be alone this Christmas.

The last armful of wood clunked noisily down onto the already large pile in the "old kitchen." It always sounded like thunder. There was a moment of silence, then the thud of the trunk lid falling shut, and finally the sound of Grandpa coming into the warmer part of the house. Those who knew him could recognize Grandpa's footsteps because of the way he limped, favoring his right leg, which had been wounded in a hunting accident when he was younger. In addition, now in his older years he was getting short-winded.

We could hear his heavy footsteps and his heavy breathing as he made his way through the door, pushing aside the quilt hanging over the doorway. Grandma turned in anticipation and went to the large doorway that separated the two rooms used during the winter. Grandpa asked, "Where shall I put it?"

"Bring it in here." she replied. He carried in a big white box with large black notes on all four sides. Stopping in the middle of the room and holding out the box, he exclaimed, "Santa Claus came early!"

He didn't have to say who it was for; I knew it was for me. Quickly I got up from the bed and took the box from Grandpa's hands. Setting it on the floor, I began nervously and excitedly to open it. Was it what I hoped it would be? Could it be what I wanted for Christmas but didn't dare to ask for because I knew it would cost too much? Tape has a way of frustrating efforts to remove it when one is anxious to open a package. Finally the tape was loosened. There in the box, to my sheer amazement, was the most beautiful red and white drum I had ever seen. Just what I wanted—and it was mine!

A mixture of feelings poured over me as I removed the drum from the box: almost overwhelming excitement from receiving a Christmas present that I had never dreamed possible, along with slight disappointment because Christmas was still a week off and I had already opened my best and maybe only present. The loneliness of David and Dorothy's absence lingered, but the warmth and love shared by my grandparents gave assurance that Christmas would be the joyous event it had been for years.

By nightfall the storm had grown worse. The wind had increased so much that the old quilt hanging over the door swayed gently with every gust of wind. The large boxelder trees just behind the house were bent so much that the limbs from the closest one rubbed on the roof. The plastic covering on the windows rustled noisily and the flame from a kerosene lamp, which Grandma had trimmed earlier that evening, flickered along with the quilt in the doorway.

Grandpa sat in his wicker rocking chair near the cookstove while Grandma sat in front of the stove, near the open oven, listening to me singing and beating on the new drum. Occasionally one of them would comment on the storm and how fortunate we were to have plenty food to eat and fuel to keep us warm. About nine o'clock, Grandma and I went to bed but Grandpa stayed up late on cold, stormy nights like this to keep the fires going in both of the stoves. It was the first night that I slept alone and in what was Dorothy's bed.

With the two kerosene lamps blown out, there was no light in the house except that which came from the fire burning in the stoves. It created shadows on the walls and ceiling of the old house, shadows that seemed alive, that kept moving and changing, reminding me of the changes which had taken place in my life that day. Changes in the weather, in feelings, in relationships; from warm to cold, from sadness to happiness, from sharing with siblings to being an only child. The day had marked a significant change in the lives of five people who lived together; now there were just the three of us.

3

By the next day the storm had subsided. Morning came early, before daylight. I was awakened every morning by the sound of Grandpa building the fires back up and making a fresh pot of coffee.

It was always comforting to hear Grandpa bring a fresh, warm cup of coffee to their bed and share it with Grandma. Grandpa would begin with some flirtatious and affectionate remark. Then he would offer Grandma a "sip" from his cup of coffee. Sometimes they would reminisce about the days when they were younger. Usually they talked about their times together before the depression, when they still had their farm. Other times they would worry about their four grandchildren and their daughter, their only living child. This morning they whispered about how David and Dorothy would get along with their father. After all, they hadn't seen each other in such a long time, and the kids were at the age when they were beginning to grow up and change rapidly. It was a real concern.

When daylight came and the sun shone brightly, Grandpa and I went outside to shovel the snow off the woodpile and clear a place to saw and split more wood. Never had I seen so much snow in all of my life! The drifts were ten to twelve feet high in places. In the fields and on the open prairie the snow was nearly three feet deep. It was so deep around the plum bushes just north of the house that only a few branches showed. And the snowdrift reached all the way down past the house, almost to the other set of plum bushes, just southwest of the house, beside the road. Only the top half of the long row of cedar trees behind the house could be seen, and the limbs on that upper half were bent low from the weight of the accumulated snow. It was an awesome sight.

Everywhere I looked the snow sparkled gold, silver, and blue. It seemed like the whole world was sparkly white and soft. Our little brown terrier—Tizer was his name—disappeared as he plunged into the snow. Only by leaping as high as he could did he come back into view, reappearing each time with a mound of soft snow on the end of his nose. There was something exciting and fun in the air this morning. I wanted to dive into the snowbank and leap around with my little brown-haired friend!

But Grandpa had other things on his mind. There was work to be done; everything else could wait until later. Grandpa was wearing his brown three-quarter-length winter coat and his matching cap, with the earflaps pulled down to keep his ears warm. He stood as straight as he could, resting his left hand on the giant scoop shovel, his other hand fisted on his hip. He too was viewing the results of the storm with an astonished look on his face. Thoughts were going through his mind that were much weightier than those which were foremost in mine. After what seemed like a long period of silence, Grandpa said, "No one will be visiting us for a while and we won't be going anyplace until the snow is blown away or packs down and hardens." With that he began to shovel a path to the woodpile.

Whenever there was a snowstorm during the night, Grandpa was always up shoveling and sweeping the snow off the porch long before daylight. This morning had been no different; the porch was nearly snowfree. It would be my job to shovel an area around both sides of the porch and a path to the outside toilet, which was near the snow-covered plum bushes north of the house. Reaching for the smaller shovel, which was leaning against the house, I paused for a moment to watch the movements and listen to sounds of Grandpa shoveling snow. There was a rhythm that left me nearly spellbound. The whispering, swishing sound of the snow sliding against his shovel came and went with each shovelful scooped up and flung to the side of the path.

It was fascinating to watch Grandpa's well-coordinated body move in a ceaseless, tireless manner. He could work for a long while before he would pause to rest. Even his breathing was synchronized with his body movements. Every time his right arm moved backward, prior to scooping up or flinging another shovelful of snow, Grandpa would inhale. When his arms moved forward, he would exhale. Inhale, exhale, inhale, exhale. Clear evidence of the virtue of experienced hard work was in motion before my eyes. It would have been easy to stand there and watch this man who even in his old age could outwork most people in this—or any—part of the country. That, however, would not get my share of the work done. I began to shovel and continued, resting for a few moments now and then, until I heard Grandpa call out, "It's about time we get something to eat. Grandma will have dinner ready pretty soon."

He was right. A short while later I finished shoveling the path to the toilet. For a few moments I watched Tizer leap through the deep, soft snow. It appeared to be a game for him to see how much snow he could pile on the end of his coal-black nose. Soon we both made our way toward the porch, where Grandpa had left his shovel and where I left mine leaning against the house. Grandpa had already gone in.

After taking off my four-buckle overshoes in the old kitchen, I carried them into the house and set them behind the cookstove to dry off so they would be warm when I was ready to go back outside. As soon as I entered the house, hunger rose within me, stirred by the wonderful and familiar scents of fried bacon, fried potatoes, and hot coffee. That was our basic diet from one day to the next, along with Grandma's homemade bread or fresh baking powder biscuits. These were the only kinds of food we could afford and could keep without electricity and modern appliances. Generally we had Jello only during the winter. Then we could put it out in the old kitchen to set, because it was always cold there. Sometimes when we were in a hurry we would set the bowl of Jello in a snowbank. There it would jell in a hurry.

As long as I lived with Grandpa and Grandma they never had a full and complete set of dishes. They only had pieces of unmatched dishes, cups, and silverware. At every meal each one of us always used the same place setting, even though none of it matched. I had my own cup, plate, and bowl, and so did Grandma and Grandpa. That's the way it had been as far back as I could remember, which was a long time. I had come to live with them five years before, when I was only three years old. It was then that Mom and Dad were divorced, and Mom was given custody of all four children. To ease her burden, we came to live with her parents. There were no legal formalities involved. They wanted us to live with them and we wanted to live with them; that was all there was to it. Since in the Indian culture grandparents are an important part of the immediate family, we thought nothing of it.

Grandpa and Grandma didn't have a complete set of dishes, and neither did they have a complete set of matching chairs; no two chairs matched. Grandpa always sat in his wicker rocking chair when we ate a meal. He was constantly sliding it back and forth from in front of the radio, where he usually sat during the day, to the kitchen table or beside the stove. Grandma sat in her straight-backed chair with the fancy spindles, using her pillow as a cushion. Always before I had sat on a homemade stool, but now that I was the only grandchild at home, I could sit on one of the other straight-backed chairs. Not only did we use the same place setting each meal and sit in the same chair, we also sat in the same place. Grandma sat near the front of the cookstove, close to the oven door, Grandpa sat near the end of the stove, and I sat between the table and the folding bed.

Grandma and Grandpa were American Indians: eating meals with them, listening to their conversation, was often delightful. Today was one of those memorable times. Grandpa began talking about his past and who he was. He had been born in a place called Northport, Michigan. There he was raised by his mother, who was Chippewa Indian, and his father, who was French. His father was a lighthouse keeper in two different locations. During the summer they lived on Fox Island and during the winter they lived in Northport. Grandpa lived in that setting with his three brothers and four sisters until he was seventeen years old. Then he decided to go away to school and learn to be an engineer. He became a student at Haskell Institute, a boarding school for American Indians in Lawrence, Kansas. His stay there was short. He couldn't accept the disregard for the students—the almost inhumane way they were treated. Soon after his arrival he and an Indian student from South Dakota ran away. They dared to do this at a time when running away from a boarding school was viewed as not unlike escaping from prison. They traveled at night and hid during the daylight hours. Grandpa "escaped" to South Dakota, where he later met my grandmother and they were married. He returned to Michigan only once, when his mother died.

All the while Grandpa was telling his story, he gazed into his green and white porcelain coffee cup, almost as though he were reading a script printed inside. He talked slowly and in a very articulate fashion, sometimes so softly I could barely hear his words. The longer he talked the softer his voice became. Only a few times did he pause long enough to take a sip from his coffee cup, which he held with both hands, shaking. After he finished, there were a few moments of silence. Then, without moving his cup, he looked up and said, "Thanks for the dinner, my dear." With that he set his cup on the table, slowly got up from his chair, and made his way back into the other room, dragging his chair behind him.

His story was like a mystery unfolding, adventure and excitement mixed with separation and sadness. It was a sadness which made it painfully difficult to talk about his home. Although he never voiced it, it was clear that Grandpa still missed his boyhood home, and may even have longed to return, if only for a brief visit. He understood what it was like to be lonesome and separated from brothers and sisters.

Grandma began to clear the table. I hurriedly put on my coat and overshoes to go outside. Pushing aside the old quilt that hung over the doorway, I made my way through the old kitchen and out onto the porch. The whole world appeared calm and quiet, the silence broken only by the flutter of wings as two ducks landed in the creek just south of the house, and the sound of that old crow calling for attention.

Today was a special day. To be sure, its meaning was much deeper than the snow.

4

Christmas came and went that year with a humble exuberance and peace, not unlike other Christmases celebrated in that little house on Choteau Creek.

In spite of the economic meagerness on which Grandma and Grandpa existed, we always had a Christmas tree with all the appropriate decorations leaning or hanging on its limbs. Somehow they always found a Christmas tree of some sort, or found the money to buy one. This year we found a tree. That wasn't the most difficult task in the world. In fact, because the snowdrift reached into the lower branches of the cedar trees behind the house, it was possible to take a good look at the tops of those trees to see which would make the nicest-looking Christmas tree. After selecting one of them, Grandpa chopped off the top with his hatchet. It was probably only about four feet tall, but to a third grader it looked much taller than that. It was my job to drag the tree back to the house, as carefully as possible. We stood it up in the corner of the porch, on the cellar door, and left it there overnight.

The same afternoon, Grandma opened her big trunk which sat

in the corner near the foot of the folding bed. That was Grandma's trunk. She had bought it many years before. In the strongest and most literal sense, that trunk "belonged" to Grandma, and nobody opened it without her permission. Even Grandpa didn't open it except to help Grandma get something out or put something in it. In that trunk Grandma stored some of her most memorable and precious belongings, including pictures of her relatives. The most impressive of these were the two large oval-shaped photographs of her uncles, her mother's cousins. There were precious pictures of Grandma and Grandpa's son, their firstborn, who had died when he was one year old. Other valuables in Grandma's trunk were contained in a shiny black chest with a white woman's picture on the cover. That chest was filled with photographs of persons who had been part of her circle of friends and extended family in years past. It was always difficult to separate the two groups, friends and extended-family members. Two empty perfume bottles, along with two old Bibles, a Book of Common Prayer, and three fancy handkerchiefs, were also kept in her trunk. That was the place where Grandma stored the decorations for the Christmas tree. It was really the only safe place in the house. There they could be stored throughout the year and not be broken.

After removing the large wooden tray from the top part of the trunk, Grandma very carefully lifted a white box from the lower section and set it on the bed. She removed the cover in an almost sacred manner. Next she turned back the soft blanket of cotton that covered the ornaments. They were as new and shiny as the year before, and the year before that one. There were five glass balls of different colors, and twelve tin twisters of different colors, each about six inches long. There was enough red crepe paper rope and silver garland to wrap around the tree about three times. In a paper sack Grandma had saved some of the thin silver strips of tinsel icicles. The moment they were uncovered, a happy anticipation came over me, as though whatever is to happen each Christmas was about to happen.

The next afternoon we were ready to put the Christmas tree up and decorate it. We had a two-gallon can that was used every year as a tree stand. I never knew what originally came in it or how long Grandpa and Grandma had it, but that is what we always used. It was filled with good black dirt, the same dirt that had been used the year before. A can of dirt was always saved because by the time we were ready to put the Christmas tree up, the ground was either frozen or covered with snow. Grandpa gingerly loosened the soil in the center. With a big spoon he carefully dug a hole large enough for the trunk of the cedar tree. Picking up the tree, he gently slid the trunk into the hole. I held the tree in place, as straight as I could, and he firmly packed the dirt around the trunk, using the handle of his big hammer. His heavy breathing indicated this wasn't easy for him to do, but he didn't seem to mind at all. Maybe he was thinking about what Christmas would have been like with just Grandma and him here. Whatever was going through his mind, he had a gleam in his eyes as he set up the Christmas tree in the old tin can.

By the time we finished securing the Christmas tree in the stand and carrying it into the house, Grandma had rearranged some of the furniture in the room where the tree was to be. The tree always sat on a table with a top that was about three feet square and with a shelf underneath, halfway down. It had spindle legs with a ball-and-claw design on the end of each. Grandma had already moved the table from behind the potbelly stove to the corner, near the radio. There it would be at a safe distance from the heat of the stove. Before the tree was set on the table, Grandma spread the white blanket of cotton on the tabletop, centering it carefully because it didn't cover the top completely. It was a beautiful tree! And its fresh spicy scent began to spread a holiday air throughout the house.

It would be my task, and mine alone this year, to decorate the tree. Standing on one of the chairs, I first hung the five glass balls on various limbs, all toward the front of the tree. Next I draped the red rope and the silver garland over the limbs and around the tree. The tin twisters were hung at the very end of twelve limbs. Finally, I placed the tinsel very sparingly and thoughtfully throughout the tree.

Just as I stepped down from the chair, Grandma came into the room. She and I stood back and gazed at the newly decorated Christmas tree. "Grandma," I said, "it looks real nice." "Yes," she replied. She stood there with me, looking at the tree even though she couldn't see very much of it. That didn't seem to matter. Because it had been decorated by her grandson, it was just right. And because her grandson was happy, she was happy. Christmas had arrived!

That evening, after we had eaten our supper and the dishes were washed, I lay on my bed while Grandma and Grandpa sat together, she on their bed and he in his rocking chair, listening to the radio. Earlier Grandma had lit both kerosene lamps and set one on the kitchen table and the other on the dresser next to my bed, as usual. Tonight, however, there were other lights in the room. The light from the lamp beside my bed reflected off each glass ball with a tiny, sharp brilliance. The same light gave a fascinating sparkle to the different-colored twisters as they turned around and around, first one way, then the other, creating a hypnotic appearance of upward and downward movement. Having never seen a Christmas tree with electric lights on it, I thought this was the most beautiful Christmas tree I had ever seen.

In what seemed like only moments it was time to go to bed. After Grandma and I were settled and Grandpa had banked the fires, he blew out the light in both the lamps and went to bed. The smell of kerosene lingered briefly, then it was gone. Even after all the lights were out and the house was dark, there were still faint reflections of light, no longer the sharp reflection of lamplight, but a soft mixture of moonlight, snow, and windows covered with plastic. In addition, the flames in the stove near my bed cast shadows of different shapes and sizes with no two figures making the same movements. They continued jumping and dancing until I fell asleep.

I was awakened in the middle of the night by the sound of the wind and Grandpa coughing. He was up again to stir the fires, shake the ashes down, and add more coal. It was a noisy but necessary procedure if we were to stay warm. Then he went back to bed, while the wind continued to blow in powerful gusts until the early hours of the morning. Grandpa said in a soft, murmuring tone, "It takes more fuel to heat the house when the wind is blowing this hard." There was no response from Grandma. Maybe she was sound asleep and Grandpa was talking to himself. Regardless, it was a concern of his. He always worried about whether or not we would have enough fuel, especially coal, to last through the winter. Soon all one could hear was the gentle purring of the fire, Grandpa snoring, and the howling of the wind outside.

The activities of the morning began before daylight. Grandma and Grandpa were already up and working in the kitchen when I woke up. On the eastern horizon one could just begin to see the various shades of red and purple in the morning sky. Christmas was just two days away. That was a thought filled with anticipation and excitement. It was a good way to begin the day. My two days alone with Grandpa and Grandma had been filled with highs and lows. No doubt today would be another day of adjustment and newness.

The lamp in the room where we slept was seldom lit in the morning, and I could not see the lamp on the kitchen table. Only the glow of lamplight could be seen through the wide opening between the two rooms. Grandpa had already moved his wicker rocking chair into the kitchen to his usual place beside the stove. From my bed all I could see was the back of his chair. Now and then the wicker made a cracking sound as he changed positions in his chair. Soon I heard the sound of Grandma's footsteps coming from the kitchen. Somehow knowing I was awake, she paused near the Christmas tree and said, "Santa Claus came during the night, and he left some things in the tree." I hurried out of bed and made my way over to the Christmas tree. There were five presents, neatly wrapped. Two of them had been placed under the tree; the other three were resting on the branches near the trunk of the tree. They would have to remain there, unopened, until Christmas morning. This Christmas was full of surprises, which made getting used to my brother's and sister's absence much easier.

After breakfast I went outside to see what the wind had done during the night. Walking out onto the porch I was astonished at the change from the day before. In the flat and open areas almost all the snow had been blown away. In some places the ground was nearly bare. But the big drifts were still there, packed down so that anybody could walk on top of them. Thoughts immediately came to mind about all the fun things I could do on those high snowbanks: slide down the huge drifts, dig tunnels through them (that was how I spent the rest of the Christmas vacation entertaining myself). There were other thoughts and feelings, too. The feeling of isolation began to subside; maybe someone would come to visit us now that so much of the snow had blown away.

On Christmas morning I carefully unwrapped my five presents from Grandma and Grandpa. We always unwrapped presents with care so Grandma could save as much of the paper as possible for the next year. The five presents I received were a handkerchief, a pair of socks, a ballpoint pen and a tablet to go with it, and a box of chocolate-covered cherries. I could expect to get those items every Christmas from then on, for the next eight years, until I was sixteen years old. I not only expected them; I looked forward to them. And the year I stopped getting them, I missed them, and did so for several years afterward.

For Grandpa and Grandma, Christmas morning came and went, as in so many other years, without any presents for them to open. I suppose this had happened for the last fifteen years, ever since the Great Depression. The only presents they received from time to time were the ones we made at school in woodwork or art classes; that was all.

Early on Christmas morning Grandpa would bring a warm, fresh cup of coffee to their bed and offer Grandma a "sip" from his cup. He would say, "Merry Christmas, my dear," and he would kiss her on her cheek. That was her Christmas present from him. His Christmas present from her was an extra-good Christmas dinner: roasted chicken with all the trimmings, including cranberries and pumpkin pie. Of course, Grandpa enjoyed and appreciated every meal that she prepared, but because Christmas dinner was extra special, both in content and in meaning, he always showed extra appreciation that day.

As I grew older, it became apparent that their Christmas gifts to each other were themselves. This enabled me to discover a much deeper meaning of Christmas—that the gift of Christmas came in the form of a person. And every year I received from them not only a handkerchief, a pair of socks, a ballpoint pen, a tablet, and a box of chocolate-covered cherries, but also the gift of Grandpa and Grandma.

5

Although Christmas had come and gone, it had left an imprint upon the heart and soul of three people who lived in that little brown house on Choteau Creek.

Traces of Christmas, of Santa Claus and grandparents, remained. The tree was still up, and when my gifts were not being used they were placed back on the table, under the tree. Leftovers of Grandma's dark, spicy pumpkin pie were still in the kitchen cabinet; the longer it sat the better it tasted, so it seemed. One or two Delicious apples still remained, a few pieces of hard candy could be found here and there, and lots of peanuts in the shell reminded us that Christmas wasn't totally over. The return to the daily routine, however, was evidence enough that it was now largely behind us.

Listening to some favorite daily radio programs was part of this routine. But first, while the sun was high, I went outside to slide down the big snowdrift on the west side of the house. It was wonderful—hard as a rock and steep too! With what seemed like great speed the sled plunged down the high drift, past the plum bushes, and on down into the middle of the pasture in front of the house. Several times I coaxed Tizer to ride with me. It was apparent from the look on his face and the stiffening of his body that he didn't enjoy the ride, but he tolerated it twice. The third time, he jumped off about halfway to the end of the long, exciting ride. He'd had enough; after that he wouldn't even run alongside the sled.

The sun was beginning to go down, and that meant it was getting near four o'clock. That was the time I had planned on going into the house. At four o'clock every weekday the radio program known as "Ma Perkins" came on. Grandma always listened to it. It was a family program, with Ma Perkins as the wise mother and grandmother who held the family together. Maybe Grandma liked the program because she could identify with Ma Perkins's role. Immediately following, the story of "Judy and Jane" could be heard. It was a romance story with a mother and her twin son and daughter as the main characters. I never knew why she liked the program except that she came to like the son. They were two of several popular soap operas on the radio at the time, and I wanted to listen to them with Grandma.

Simply going into the house involved a long and (to an eight-year-old) unnecessary process. While still on the porch, I took the broom and began sweeping off all the snow that had accumulated on my overshoes, overalls, and coat and mittens. Some of it had frozen on. It would melt off after I was in the house a few minutes, but it would leave my pants legs wet. That is what Grandpa didn't want to happen, although it didn't matter to me. During the winter I always wore two pair of overalls for warmth, so I really didn't feel the dampness very much. But Grandpa was pretty strict about such things. He would say, "You'll catch a cold, going around like that."

After sweeping off all the loose snow, I went into the old kitchen. There I removed my overshoes and unbuttoned my coat before entering the main part of the house. As soon as I pushed

33

back the old quilt covering the doorway, I could feel that warm air against my face in sharp contrast to the cold, brisk wind I had just come in from. But something else was noticeably different: the radio was not turned on. Ordinarily Grandma turned on the radio several minutes before her programs began. Something was wrong; I could feel it in the air and in my very being. Making my way around the kitchen stove, I nervously stood in the doorway between the two rooms. Grandma sat in Grandpa's rocking chair with her back to me and her eyes fixed upon Grandpa; both of her elbows rested on her knees. Grandpa was sitting on the edge of their bed holding a wet washcloth over his nose.

"What's wrong?" I exclaimed. "What happened?" Grandpa looked up, his big eyes appearing even bigger because the rest of his face was hidden behind the washcloth. Removing the washcloth from his nose, he answered in a reassuring and confident manner, "My nose is bleeding, but it will be all right." With that he covered his nose again. One didn't have to look very long or close to know that his nose was bleeding hard.

Grandma turned toward me and said, "His nose started to bleed about an hour ago and he can't get it to stop. Maybe we will have to take him to the hospital." That was a frightening thought. When Grandma and Grandpa went to see a doctor, they went to the nearest Public Health hospital, which was about eighteen miles away. I began to ask myself questions, one after another: How would we get him there? Who would take him to the hospital? Could anybody make it down to the house in a car?

For the next hour or so we continued to give Grandpa fresh washcloths, rinsing out one while he used the other. The bleeding did not seem to slow down. He tried to lie down for a while, but every time he began to fall asleep he would choke from the blood dripping down into his throat. Finally he sat in his rocking chair, leaned back, and held the cold, wet washcloth over his nose.

34

After several minutes of this, Grandpa instructed Grandma and me to get the old ash pan, put some ashes in it, and bring it to him. Without putting on my coat and overshoes, I went into the old kitchen and found the pan to which he was referring, then went out to the ash pile, following the path Grandpa had shoveled several days before. With an empty coffee can I put several scoops of ashes into the big pan, until they covered the entire bottom. I ran back into the house, carefully carrying the pan so that the ashes would not blow into my face. At the same time, I ran as fast as I could because I was chilled to the bone and because there was a real sense of urgency about all that was happening. When I returned, Grandpa told me to set the pan on the floor in front of him, between his feet. Then he leaned forward, removed the washcloth from his nose, and began to let the blood drip into the pan of ashes. After rinsing out his washcloth, I sat on his and Grandma's bed, almost directly in front of him, and just watched for a few moments. Thinking this could go on all night, I glanced out the window to the east; it was already dark outside. For a few moments there was nobody else in the whole world but me and Grandpa. I wanted to put my arms around him and tell him how much I loved him, but this didn't seem like the time to do it. He just sat there, looking down, with his hands on his knees. And there was the steady drip of blood falling off the end of his nose into the pan of ashes.

Suddenly I became aware that Grandma was fixing supper. She was warming the leftovers from the day before. Before she set the table, she asked, "Billie, are you going to be able to eat some supper?" Without looking up, and shaking his head only slightly from side to side, he answered, "No, you two go ahead and eat. Maybe I'll have a biscuit later on tonight." He seemed to think that the bleeding would stop later, during the night—or was he just hoping?

When supper was ready, Grandma and I sat down to eat. We

sat across from each other, separated by the table, with the kerosene lamp in the middle and off to the side. There was little conversation, just an occasional glance in the direction where Grandpa was sitting quietly and motionlessly. We seemed to be eating not because we were hungry, but because it was time to eat and something to do while we waited. For sure, this would be an anxious night.

Grandma's face had a worried look. She was a person with a tremendously strong and constant faith in God and in life. She accepted all sorts of events and happenings in life in such a way that she demonstrated this faith to those around her. There were times, however, when Grandma evidenced a kind of awareness that whatever had happened or was about to happen would have serious consequences. This was one of those times, for Grandma had a deep crease in her forehead. It was the mark that made those who knew her well realize she believed she had good reason to worry.

The radio was not turned on at all the entire evening. The house was quiet and tense as we sat with Grandpa, and waited, and prayed. No one listened to the six o'clock news, or the Bohemian Band, or any other evening program, as we normally did. All was quiet. Even the wind outside had grown calm and still. All one could hear was the drip, drip, drip of Grandpa's nose bleeding.

I remember Grandpa teaching me, long before, how to build a fire in either stove safely, and how to shake the ashes down, just how to replenish the fire with the right amount of fuel, and how to control the flames through the use of various drafts and dampers. Tonight it was my responsibility to use what he had taught me. Before Grandma and I went to bed, I brought in a fresh box of corncobs, an armful of split wood, and a scuttleful of coal from the old kitchen. After building the fire up in both stoves, then closing the drafts and dampers, I got ready for bed.

Grandpa said he was going to move his chair behind the potbelly stove and sit there until his nose stopped bleeding. I helped him move his chair and the pan of ashes to where he was going to sit. Before I crawled into bed, I blew out the lamp in the kitchen, then I turned down the light in the lamp beside my bed as low as possible. I was determined that I would stay awake as long as Grandpa had to sit up, but soon I was overcome by sleep.

Sometime during the night I heard the voice of a man calling out. Both Grandma and I woke up at the same time and realized that it was Grandpa's voice we heard. Both of us responded to him at the same time. He had fallen asleep in his chair and was having a nightmare. By this time there was a large blood stain on the bib of his overalls. After he woke up and realized what had happened, he assured us that he was all right and told us to go back to sleep. I was able to do so, but not Grandma, because I vaguely remember turning over at times during the rest of the night and seeing and hearing her up with Grandpa.

Very early the next morning, before daylight, Grandma came to my bed to awaken me. Before she got there, however, I was awake. Very calmly she said, "You better get up and go to the Satlers' and have them call your Uncle Jim. Have him come to take your Grandpa to the hospital. He feels weak and dizzy."

Before she was through talking, I was up and dressing. Without bothering to wash my face, I slipped on my overshoes, coat, and mittens, and was out the door and off the porch. So quickly did I move that I startled the dogs, and all three of them started barking and running in different directions, as though they were looking for something to attack. As fast as I could I ran down to the creek, across the ice, and up the bank where I had last seen David and Dorothy the day they left.

From the top of the bank I could see the Satlers' barn and the house where they lived. Before I could get to their house I had to go through their barnyard. Just outside the gate stood their whole herd of cows, waiting to be milked. Light was beginning to creep into the eastern sky. It was still dark enough, though, that I could not tell one cow from another, and somewhere in the midst of that herd was a huge bull. The Satlers weren't up yet; at least I couldn't see a light in their house. If their bull decided to attack, there would be no one near to help. But there was no time to worry of such things; Grandpa was sick and needed help now. Even so, my heart began to pound inside of me. I could feel it pounding as I began to breathe deeply. I continued to walk at a fast pace. Halfway through the herd, there he was, standing to my right, over by the fence. I stopped, but only for a moment, then I continued to walk even faster toward the gate. The bull just stood there, watching me walk through the herd and climb over the gate. I breathed a sigh of relief. Had the bull even moved, I would have started to cry.

With that behind me, at least for the moment, I ran through the barnyard to the house and knocked on the front door. After knocking a few times, pausing in between, I waited, watching for a light and listening for sounds of life inside the house. Soon Art came to the door. I quickly explained to him why I was there—that Grandpa was sick and wanted them to call Uncle Jim and tell him to come to take Grandpa to the hospital. In a few brief moments I heard Art saying to someone on the phone, "I think you can make it to the house by coming over the Black Bridge and going through the fields north of the house. Take down any fence of mine that you need to in order to get to the house and get him to the hospital." With that he hung up. Turning to me, he said, "They will be there as soon as possible."

Uncle Jim was Grandpa's younger brother. He too had come to South Dakota when he was young, had married a poor widow with seven children, and stayed for the rest of his life. He and several of his stepchildren came to visit Grandpa and Grandma regularly, especially during the summer when the roads were dry.

38

Coming all the way to the house in a car would not be an easy task for them this morning, but Uncle Jim was a daring person; he and Grandpa came from the same stock. If there was a way for them to do it, they would find that way.

I made my way back through the barnyard, again watching for the bull in the herd. By then he had gone to the other side of the barn, which was quite a distance from the gate. This time I crawled under the gate and ran down to and across the creek and home again. By the time I got home, Grandpa had managed to change his clothes and was once more sitting behind the potbelly stove, allowing his nose to drip into the ashes. Grandma was also ready and waiting for my return with some word.

In less than an hour Uncle Jim and Kenneth, his oldest stepson, drove up almost to the front of the house. They came in for just a few minutes. Meanwhile, I got Grandpa a coffee can half filled with fresh ashes, which he took with him. I had never seen Grandpa so pale. He was, as he would have said, "as white as a sheet." They were ready to go. I, however, decided to stay home alone. While Uncle Jim did not approve of it, he assured me that they wouldn't be gone too long. In spite of his weakness and dizziness, Grandpa put his arm around me and said, "My boy, don't worry. I'll be back. Take good care of things while I'm gone." With that he put on his hat and coat and went out the door with Grandma close behind him.

A short while after lunch they returned, but Grandpa was not with them. Uncle Jim explained that because Grandpa had lost so much blood, he had to stay in the hospital to be built back up. He went on, "The doctor said we got him there just in time." After having a cup of coffee and a few of Grandma's homemade cookies, Uncle Jim and Kenneth left.

That night Grandma and I were very much aware that we were alone. Grandpa's presence was missed by both of us. I kept the fires going; Grandma sat in front of the oven with her left arm crossed in front of her and her right elbow resting on her left hand, while her right hand covered her eyes and her forehead. Grandma sat there with her eyes closed, as she did so often, in deep thought. Night after night she sat in that place, in that position, her right hand over her forehead and her eyes closed. Sometime she would talk about her life as a child, living with her parents. Other times, she would dramatically tell stories from the Bible, especially the Old Testament.

Tonight, however, she was thinking about Grandpa. After a long period of silence, which was not unusual for her and others in our Indian culture, she began to speak without looking up. "Several nights ago," she said, "I woke up in the middle of the night. There was an owl on the roof of the house. It continued to make noise, very loud. When an owl lands on a house," she continued, "it brings bad news to those who live there. It means that sickness or tragedy will come to that house. I worried about your mother in the big city. I never dreamed it was your Grandpa it was talking about."

That night I went to bed thinking about the deep crease in Grandma's forehead the day before. She knew she had good reason to worry. The owl had warned her. Before going to sleep, I wondered about the seriousness of Grandpa's illness and what was in store for us. The owl seemed to know.

6

The house was very quiet after Grandpa went into the hospital. It was especially quiet during the early-morning hours when he usually built the fires and made a fresh pot of coffee. Since he was not at home, some of this responsibility was mine. The first thing that Grandpa did when he got up in the morning was to look at the thermometer on the wall above the radio. He would quickly check the room temperature, using the light from his flashlight. Then he started the fires and made coffee. Once the thermometer registered about seventy-eight degrees, then it was all right for Grandma to get out of bed and start her day.

Like Grandpa, I started the fire in the kitchen stove by using the dried corncobs dipped in kerosene. Once that fire was started, I then shook the ashes down in the potbelly stove and built that fire back up. Next I made a pot of coffee for Grandma and me. It gave an eight-year-old an adult feeling. When I really felt, if not adult-like, at least like a big person, was when we would get ready for bed. I was the last person in bed; therefore, I blew out the light in the lamp. Grandma and I got along well those first few days, even though we both missed the man of the house.

Several days after Grandpa had gone into the hospital, Uncle Jim and Kenneth came again, to take Grandma and me to visit Grandpa. Again, for some unexplainable reason, I didn't want to go. And Uncle Jim was not too pleased with the idea of my staying home alone. But Grandma said it was all right, so her word prevailed. After having a quick cup of coffee, they were gone, making their way over the hills, on the back roads, across the fields, around the drifts and other places where the snow was deep.

The house had been quiet before, but now that Grandma was gone it was even quieter. Glancing out the window and seeing the sun shining brightly, I said to myself, "It is a good day for them to visit Grandpa." The thought even occurred to me that he might be well enough to come home with them. I knew, of course, that they wouldn't be home until late afternoon, because Grandma had planned on seeing the doctor while she was there, in order to get some of her medicines replenished. Since there was always a long line of people waiting to see the doctor, that could take most of the afternoon.

Not more than an hour after they had gone, the dogs began to bark, like someone they recognized was coming. A short while later there was a knock on the outside door. Naturally, I wondered who it was. No fear rose within me, not even a little bit of nervousness. Only a few people came to visit, especially at this time of the year—people who needed to borrow some very basic food, or someone who was concerned about how Grandpa and Grandma were getting along. There was no one in the whole countryside of whom I should be afraid. Opening the door, I saw Tommy standing there on the porch. As always, I was glad to see him.

I had known Tommy all of my life. He was about forty-two years old, some five feet eight inches tall, and weighed about one hundred and fifty pounds. He had thick black hair with streaks of silver shining through. He was a man with a relatively small face which was made even more apparent by his crushed jaw. When he was a teenager, he was kicked in the jaw by one of his father's horses. It was crushed and never rebuilt. Even as I had known Tommy all of my life, Tommy had known Grandpa and Grandma all of his life. In fact, Grandma and his mother had gone to the same boarding school when they were young. He always referred to them as Uncle Bill and Aunt Bessie. Years before, he had been married and partially raised four children, then he and his wife were divorced. I never knew his wife and barely knew his children, who came to visit him from Chicago once in a while.

His only source of income was working for various farmers nearby. He evidently was a good worker, since he was always in demand during the planting and harvest seasons. During those times he worked all week, then went to town on the weekend to get drunk. Almost every Saturday night, about one o'clock in the morning, the dogs would begin to bark. It would be Tommy coming to bring his "Uncle Bill" a drink. Grandpa would get up and have a couple tastes of wine with him while Grandma made a bed in which he would sleep. Generally he would stay all day Sunday and listen to the ball game on the radio with Grandpa. Late in the afternoon, when he was completely sober, he would play catch with me, run races with me, or just sit and tell stories and jokes. He was a significant person in my life. There was only one Tommy in the world, and I loved him very much.

During the winter months Tommy lived with his mother. Because there was no work available for him then, he would come to visit my grandparents and sometimes stayed for days. He helped Grandpa and me shovel snow and chop and saw wood. Once when the winter was long and fierce and there was no way for Grandpa and Grandma to go to town, Tommy walked almost all the nine miles to Avon and back in order to get them the groceries they needed. Tommy was one of the very few persons who came to visit us because he really cared and was concerned.

After a brief greeting I invited him in. As soon as he entered the house, he asked, "Where is Uncle Bill and Aunt Bessie?" After we sat down I told him the whole story of how Grandpa's nose bled all night, and how I went to the Satlers' to call Uncle Jim. By the time I finished, he decided to wait until Grandma came back, in order to find out how "Uncle Bill was feeling." With that I poured each of us a cup of coffee, and we began to visit, telling stories and jokes and laughing about life. It was a good day. Tommy helped me to let go of my worry about Grandpa's health, at least for a few hours.

One did not have to look out the window very long to notice that the sun was beginning its descent toward the western horizon and shadows were beginning to lengthen like fingers of different shapes reaching toward the east. It won't be long before the cold night air will permeate the land. The animals will soon be coming out of their dens and places of shelter to hunt and play. There was another feeling in the air, as though something was not right but that in the end everything would work out.

The minutes ticked away on the big round-faced clock that sat on the radio and still there was no sign of Uncle Jim and Kenneth bringing Grandma back home. Even though we continued to visit and enjoy each other's company, it was clear that both Tommy and I were beginning to feel uneasy.

Then there were the welcoming sounds of the dogs barking. Either an animal was passing by or someone was coming; we hoped it was the latter. Immediately I went out on the porch to see why they were barking. By this time the sky was still light but the earth was darkening rapidly. First there was the sound of an automobile making its way through the field in back of the house to the north. It was difficult to tell if the car was near or still faraway, since sounds carried far and easily in the night air. Only a few moments later, beams of light shone over the dark horizon. I assumed it was them, because no one else knew how to get to the house from that direction.

When the car stopped near the house, I could see there were only two people in it. Uncle Jim got out and walked toward the porch, while Kenneth remained seated on the driver's side. "They kept Bess in the hospital," he said. That was all he said as he walked into the house with me following close behind. On entering the house, I could hear Uncle Jim's loud voice say, "Hi, Tom." "Hi, Jim," came the softer reply. After sitting down in Grandpa's rocking chair, which we had moved into the kitchen, near the stove, Uncle Jim said to me in a much quieter voice, "After the doctor saw her, he wanted to keep her for a few days . . . nothing serious. So we thought you should go home with us until one of them gets out." Uncle Jim had no sooner stopped talking than Tommy said, "Or I can stay here with him."

It was strange, Uncle Jim's reaction. He didn't even give me a chance to decide. He probably knew I would chose to stay home, with Tommy there. He stood up and said, "In a few days we'll go back to see how they're doing." That was all. He didn't even ask if I would like to ride along. He just got up from his chair, spoke his few words, and left. During a time of uncertainty and instability, I must have unknowingly evidenced finding comfort and security in that old house. There was the sound of a car door closing, the starting of the engine, and they were gone.

It was not until then that I noticed the house was getting dark and it was time to light at least one lamp. If I hurried, we could eat supper and get the dishes washed before the six o'clock news. Together we prepared our supper. Tommy sliced the bacon while I set the table. I fried the bacon and eggs while Tommy kept the fire burning with a steady but low flame. We were fortunate that there was plenty of Grandma's homemade bread left from the last time she baked. She always made a big batch of loaves and biscuits.

Sometimes the loaves of bread would get pretty dry before we ate them. With the food ready, we sat down to eat. I assumed the responsibility of saying the grace. I used the grace that I had heard Grandpa say hundreds of times, and so had Tommy: "O Lord, we thank you for this food. Bless it to our use and us to thy service, through Christ our Lord. Amen." We visited all through the meal. It was amazing how many different things we could think of to talk about.

When supper was over, the dishes were stacked and set to one side to make room for the dishpan. Actually, there were three different pans that were placed on the table: one to wash in, one to rinse in, and one to drain in. The dishpan was the largest. It was made of porcelain. The rinsing pan was a smaller porcelain bowl. The pan that was used to drain the dishes in was a round, shallow, flat tin cover that looked like today's pizza pans. Half of the hot water from the large goosenecked aluminum teakettle was poured into the dishpan, and the rest into the rinse pan. Cups and glasses were always washed first. Whoever was drying the dishes always left one cup in the drain pan to lean the dishes on while they dripped and drained.

Having finished with supper and the dishes in time, we listened to three programs on the radio that night: the six o'clock news, the Bohemian Band, and the Lone Ranger. Within an hour they were over with. For the next several hours we sat in the kitchen talking about everything and anything. The night went by fast.

The next morning Tommy was up first, but not as early as Grandpa usually got up. Tommy built the fires that warmed the house. After a quick breakfast we chopped some wood and carried it into the old kitchen, where it was neatly stacked. Whenever Tommy did something he always left things looking neat and clean. When we were almost finished, the dogs began to bark and run up the hill toward the west. We stopped to watch and listen. We could hear a car coming toward the house, using the back road that Uncle Jim and Kenneth had formed. A few moments later a black car appeared over the top of the hill and made its way down to the house. It was the Episcopal priest, Father Cyril Rouillard. He was a member of the Santee Sioux Tribe with its reservation on the Nebraska side of the Missouri River. He was not very tall but very distinguished-looking man, neatly dressed in black with a white clerical collar, all of which blended nicely with his thick, coarse black hair that had a tint of gray shining through. He always wore a cross on a beaded chain with special American Indian designs on it. His smile and gentle voice were enough to warm the weather and make his presence welcome in anybody's life. He was very much loved by the people in the tiny mission church where we worshiped.

This day Father Rouillard came to visit and bring Holy Communion to Grandpa and Grandma and whoever else was at the house. Pausing to visit outside the house for what was to be just a few minutes, he asked how they were. When I told him what had happened, he was quite surprised and very concerned about everyone, including me. He said, "Then I will go to the hospital to see them." And he was gone. How he ever happened upon that back road was more than either Tommy or I could figure out. We felt it was too bad Father Rouillard had not found Grandpa and Grandma at home, since a minister or a priest very seldom came to visit.

"I'll tell you what," said Tommy with a smile on his face. "After lunch, let's go spear some fish." That, I thought, was a good idea. After putting together a quick and meager lunch, we took the ax and the spear and walked down to the creek. It was a sunny day, just like the day when David and Dorothy left. Once again I could hear the rippling sound of the water flowing over the rocks where the stream was shallow. The ice never froze over there. It stirred some lonely feelings within me. But there was no time for that; we had fish to spear for supper.

Tommy began chopping a hole in the ice, probably about two feet wide and six feet long, across the creek, where he figured the water wasn't very deep. It was fun to watch him cut into three pieces the one big chunk of ice he had just loosened, then hook each piece with the ax and slide it out of the hole and onto the surrounding ice. He knew how to do it in such a way that it looked very easy. Next he took the spear and carefully scooped the smaller pieces of ice out of the water until the opening was nearly ice-free. I could see the very bottom of the creek, the water was so clear. Taking several handfuls of dried corn out of his pocket, he dropped them evenly into the water and we watched each kernel settle to the bottom. This created a lighter background in the water which made it easier to see the fish go by. As we stood there looking down into the water, facing downstream, we could see hundreds of tiny fish swim by so fast that it was impossible to tell what kind they were. It seemed the smaller they were, the faster they moved. This meant, of course, that the large fish, which were carp, would swim by very slowly. Even though I had seen this phenomenon before, experiencing it with Tommy was especially fun.

I took the ax and walked upstream, around the bend, which went northeast of the house. After going a quarter of a mile, I began to make my way slowly back toward the place where Tommy was standing by the ice hole with the spear in his hand about an inch above the water, waiting for a big fish to swim by. Using the ax, I tapped on the ice, zigzagging back and forth across the creek. When I came around the bend, I could see three large fish lying on the ice. Tommy plunged his spear into the water again, as swift as an arrow. From where I was standing, I could see the very top of the spear handle wiggling. Tommy firmly held the spear down in the water. After a few moments he

48

flipped another big carp onto the ice, far enough away from the hole so it couldn't flop its way back into the water. I couldn't believe my eyes.

Tommy looked back and motioned for me to come quickly. Before I reached where he was standing, he held the spear out to me and whispered, "Here, you try it." I didn't say a word. All I could think was "Wow!"

I stood there with my back upstream so the fish, swimming downstream, couldn't see me holding the spear just above the water. Tommy stood beside me. "There goes one!" he said. But I was too excited to move. Very softly he said, "You have to move quickly." At that moment another big fish went swimming by, and over to my right another one. Immediately below my spear was still another one. I plunged the spear into the water. I could feel the strength of the fish struggling against the spear. Tommy knew I had it. In a louder voice he said, "Hold it down until it stops fighting, then flip it up on the ice." I waited and waited. I wanted to be sure. This was my first one and I didn't want to lose it. Finally I flipped it out of the water onto the ice. It was heavy and it was big. It wasn't the largest catch of the day, but it was big and it was my first, and that was good enough for me!

Tommy said, "It's time to go home and clean these fish." I wasn't ready to go, but I knew he was right. He took out his jackknife and cut a long, skinny limb off a tree. Then he trimmed off every branch except the last and largest one. He cut that one off about six inches from the limb. He threaded the small end of the limb into the gills of each fish and out the mouth. There were five large carp on that limb, and it was heavy. Tommy took the ax and fish while I carried the spear, and up the bank and home we went as the sun began to go down. We had to hurry if we were going to clean and skin our catch before it got dark. And we did. The last fish was cleaned and skinned before the evening sun touched the western horizon. Tommy did all the work; I just watched. But he made me feel like these were *our* fish and *we* had cleaned them.

No sooner had we gone into the house than the dogs began to bark and run up the hill. Before I could go out to see what they were barking at, I heard car doors slamming shut. Going out onto the porch, I was overcome with emotion. There was Uncle Jim and Kenneth. And right behind them came Grandpa and Grandma! The day had been filled with so much fun that it hadn't mattered that Grandpa and Grandma weren't home. Once I laid eyes on them, however, I realized how much I had missed them. Grandpa hugged me and asked, "How's my boy?" I couldn't answer him. Then Grandma also hugged me and said, "Here's my little boy." We all went into the house.

With no west windows, it got dark in the house early, so I proceeded to light both lamps. Suddenly the dogs began to bark once more. Going out to investigate, I saw to my surprise another car coming down the hill. It was Father Rouillard. He got halfway out of his car and asked, "Did your grandparents make it home?" When I answered, "Yes," he closed the car door and came to the house. I invited him in. He walked in with his little black suitcase. Setting it down, he shook the hand of everyone in the house. When he shook Grandpa's hand, he said, "I finally caught up with you." They both laughed. Then he said, "I came to celebrate Holy Communion with you." Grandpa answered, "That is just fine." Father Rouillard began to lay out the communion supplies on the dresser next to my bed.

Only seconds later Uncle Jim said, "Well, Kenneth, don't you think we ought to go?" Kenneth agreed. Grandpa thanked him for everything. They shook each other's hand, and Uncle Jim and Kenneth left. I suppose Uncle Jim and Kenneth, being Catholic, felt uncomfortable when Father Rouillard said we would celebrate Holy Communion. After they were gone, we all received our communion. The ritual was short but meaningful.

Grandma wouldn't have been herself if she didn't invite Father Rouillard to stay for supper. They spoke in Dakota. Grandma said, "Htayetuwota iyanka" ("Stay for supper"). He responded by saying, "Hau, pidamaya" ("Yes, thank you"). At that she began to prepare the meal. In what seemed like just a few minutes, the five of us were gathered around the kitchen table relishing fresh fried fish, potatoes fried with onion, sliced homemade bread, and fresh, hot coffee. We had celebrated the Lord's Supper, and now we were celebrating another supper that was equally as tender and redemptive. It was homecoming.

The next morning Tommy returned to his home. Before he left, Grandma thanked him for staying with me and helping out. I followed him out the door and stood on the porch, watching him walk up the hill and out of sight. We had had a good time together. During the past few days I had grown a little, learned how to assume responsibility, and become more aware of just how much Grandpa and Grandma meant to me.

In the field, a short distance from the house, I could hear a rooster pheasant crowing. Tomorrow would be New Year's Eve. Soon it would be time to go back to school. We hadn't heard from David and Dorothy since they left. If they didn't come back, that would mean I would have to walk to and from school alone. I knew I could do that. For sure, I also knew, things would be different from now on.

7

The winters were long and harsh out on the Dakota prairie. The wind would blow night after night, day in and day out. Usually the strong winds came from the northwest. Occasionally, when the wind blew from the northeast, Grandpa would say, "The weather is going to be real cold for the next few days." That gave us all the more reason to store up wood and corncobs in the old kitchen, and he would say, "I suppose I won't get much sleep tonight. I'll probably be up most of the night keeping the fires going." There were times when he did stay up during the night in order to keep that old house thawed out. There were a few bitter cold nights when he fell asleep and slept longer than he had intended. When he woke up, the thermometer in the house measured way below freezing, so far below that the water in the basin and the galvanized pail on the washstand had a layer of ice an inch thick.

We were not the only ones, however, who felt the brunt of the winter, and both Grandpa and Grandma were very much aware of what was going on around us. Several times a day they would turn on the old pack-battery-run radio and listen to the news and the weather report. Even though they seldom went anywhere, they always listened to the cancellations, especially the school closings. Perhaps they gauged the severity of the weather by the number and kinds of cancellations. Sometimes events were canceled due to a snowstorm and other times they were canceled due to the extreme cold.

One severe snowstorm during the winter of 1949 lasted for several days and was followed by another, and another, with only one or two days in between. Grandpa kept his ear to the radio during this time. The reports were that the farmers' cattle throughout the area were dying. They were freezing to death. Some of them apparently became snow blind and wandered off in the storm. They would get stuck in some big snowdrift and freeze, or they would fall through the ice on some creek and drown. At one point it was reported on the six o'clock news that the Red Cross was dropping bales of hay from airplanes into pastures where livestock huddled together, stranded in fields across the state.

With every snowstorm the already huge snowdrifts grew larger and were packed down and frozen as solid as a rock. On my way to and from school I walked up and down the snowdrifts, which dotted the prairie like little rolling hills. They accumulated so high that I could easily touch the telephone wires. Some places I appeared taller than the telephone poles, for only the very tops stood above the drifts.

Wild animals struggled for survival, too. Pheasants and other birds died from the cold or starved because too much snow had covered their source of food. The evidences of wolves were more numerous than most people could remember. Everyone was aware that wolves roamed the countryside, but very seldom were they seen and only occasionally did they cause problems. This winter, however, the wolves came out of their dens at night and attacked the livestock that were stranded in pastures, too far from the safety of their barnyards.

Some said it was the worst winter of the century. It was the worst winter I had ever seen, that was for sure. There was grave concern for the welfare of people who lived a long distance from the roads where the snowplow went through. Although we didn't know it, we were one of those families, since we lived nearly two miles from the next county road. At first the weather and our isolation didn't seem to worry Grandpa and Grandma. After all, we had plenty of food and fuel to last for a while. The storms, however, didn't let up, and Grandpa began to show some concern. "With this steady wind and cold," he said, "we are burning more fuel than usual. I hope we have enough to last." Then the end of the month drew near. That was when meals were carefully planned by Grandma in order to make the remaining food last until she and Grandpa went to town again. This month there was evidence of growing anxiety in the rationing of food at each meal. Grandpa and Grandma agreed to make the coffee weak and to use less sugar and cream so they would last longer. It was apparent to all of us that we wouldn't be going to town as we usually did along about the third of the month. In fact, Grandpa began to wonder if we would get to town at all during the next month, especially if the weather continued as it had for the past several weeks.

The severe weather didn't let up over the next few weeks. When we were about a week past the time when Grandpa and Grandma normally went to town, we were out of a variety of foods. We were living on weak coffee, cornmeal mush, baking powder biscuits, and slices of bacon from a slab that was nearly all fat. Grandma worried about the food, while Grandpa was more concerned about having enough fuel for the rest of the winter.

One night the wind and snow did cease. The sky was as clear as could be, with stars brightly shining like diamonds in the sky. Grandpa said, "It's going to be another cold night, but at least the wind has stopped blowing. That will help save on fuel." He was right: it was a very cold night, and he was up several times banking the fires.

The next morning the sky was still clear and the wind was very calm. Although the sun shone brightly throughout the day, the temperature didn't rise above zero. Several times during the day I went out on the porch and just stood there looking around. The floor in the old kitchen and the boards on the porch cracked beneath my feet from the constant extremely cold temperatures. After sharing a meager supper, I once more put on my coat and went outside. The evening sun was beginning to set in the southwestern horizon. It was as red as fire. Within a few moments the cold pierced my coat and gloves. Then I heard the sound of an airplane. Glancing around, I could see a small plane with skis, flying unusually low south of the house. It appeared to be following the creek, which made me think it was the game warden on his beat. After the plane passed the house and made its way to the southeast, away from the house, it suddenly turned and came straight toward the house. I stood there watching, almost stunned. To my surprise, it landed in the pasture and continued to make its way toward the house.

I hurried inside to tell Grandpa and Grandma about it, I was so excited. At first they didn't believe me. Then they saw just how excited I really was. Grandma went back out on the porch with me to see what was going on. By the time we got there, the plane had stopped and the pilot was already out of it and trying to make his way to the house. He was a big man and wore a heavy sheepskin coat, hat, and gloves, as well as snow boots that were also lined with sheepskin. When he got to the porch, he introduced himself and explained that he represented the Red Cross. He asked if he could come into the house for a few minutes. Of course Grandma invited him in and even poured a cup of weak coffee for him. He had come from the town of Wagner, which was about sixteen miles northwest of where we lived. He said, "Your name was given to me and I was asked to come and see if you people are all right, and to find out if you need any groceries. If you do," he went on, "I will be glad to get them and bring them to you in the morning." Immediately Grandpa said, "Well, we could use a few groceries, but we don't have any money here with us." "That's all right," the man replied; "the Red Cross will pay for any groceries you need."

It took only a glance at Grandma to see the look of relief on her face. In her modest way she said, "Yes, there are a few things that we are almost out of." Looking in her direction, the man said, "Make a list of the things you need and I'll be glad to get them for you." Grandma got out her tablet and her indelible pencil and began to write. It was a short list. It contained only enough items to get us through. She included things like coffee, sugar, canned milk, baking powder, oatmeal, yeast, and shortening. Quickly scanning over the list, he asked, "Do you have plenty of flour?" Grandma pointed to a small bag in the corner and answered, "Well, I have this much left." Without any hesitation he said, "Maybe you better add that to your list." She did.

Before he left, he inquired about others who lived out in the country and might need some assistance. Grandma and Grandpa gave him the names of other Indian families in the area and told him where they lived. Within a few moments he finished his coffee and thanked Grandma for it and was out the door. All three of us followed him out and watched him turn the propeller to start the airplane's engine and climb into the cockpit. He slowly taxied out into the pasture southeast of the house, the same place where he had landed. He turned the plane in the direction of the house, revved the engine, and began picking up speed while traveling straight toward the front porch. Before he got near, the plane lifted high above the house, like a giant yellow bird. All three of us waved to him as he flew over the house. We could see him wave and he dipped the wings of the airplane several times. In a few moments the plane was out of sight. We all went back into the house, still hardly believing what we had experienced, it had all happen so fast. We looked forward to his return in the morning.

That evening the wind came up again, yet a stillness permeated the house in spite of the howling north wind and all the sounds that come from an old house withstanding its force. The walls would crack now and then, the sound echoing across the high ceiling. The plastic coverings on the windows rattled and sometimes popped so loudly it seemed as though they wouldn't be in place by morning. With every burst of wind the branches of the old boxelder trees behind the house rustled and squeaked as the limbs rubbed against each other. The old quilt hanging across the doorway swayed slightly with each gust, an indication of how much wind was forcing its way into the old kitchen and around the edges of the door to the room in which we sat. The flame in the kerosene lamp sitting in the center of the kitchen table flickered in response to the breath of old man winter. The fires purred within the cookstove and the potbelly stove and up the chimneys. From time to time something would pop inside the kitchen stove as though someone had dropped a kernel of popcorn into the fire. One of the cats sat on the cellar door outside, begging to come into the house. Without looking up or moving her hand away from her forehead, Grandma broke the silence by saying, "He can go under the house if he gets cold." It was as though she knew what I was thinking at that moment. Or perhaps we were both thinking the same thing. There was more silence, broken only by the rhythmic sound of the spirit that moves the clouds and sways the trees.

Grandma was silent again for a long while. Maybe she was

thinking about her parents and some of the precious and sometimes mysterious experiences they shared together. Like the time when she was about eight years old and her father was building a fireplace. He had recently finished building the log house Grandma was raised in. The fireplace was at the north end of the house. It was completed enough that Grandma's mother could use it for cooking. The only thing her father had left to finish was the outside of the chimney, up above the roof. He would go to a certain place about a mile and a half away, along the Missouri River, to get the clay he used in constructing the fireplace. On this particular day her mother was sitting near the fire, for she was keeping a close watch on something she was cooking. All of a sudden pieces of clay began to fall down the chimney, bouncing off the covered kettle and into the fire. The cover on the kettle rattled as more clay came down the chimney. Her first and immediate thought was that her husband was teasing her. She leaned forward and looking up the chimney she said, "Heconśni, witkotkoka" ("Stop acting foolishly"). She waited and listened for a while, thinking he would respond with laughter or some more foolishness. But there was no response. So she went outside to make sure he was all right. Looking up toward the chimney, she saw no one there. She hurried around to the back of the house, but he was nowhere to be found.

Half an hour or so later Grandma's father came rushing into the house. The first thing he wanted to know was whether everyone was okay. He quickly told his story. "I ran out of clay," he said, "so I went to the river to get some more. I climbed halfway down the bank and was digging the clay. All of a sudden the whole river bank began to shake! It shook so much," he said, "that I nearly fell off it and into the river! I got scared so I came home as fast as I could."

Several weeks later the rumor reached their house that there had been an earthquake in Nebraska about this same time, around the year 1885. Grandma told this story many, many times, but it never got old. The way she told it, it was always fresh and apparently vividly etched into her mind.

There was more silence. Now, however, it was a silence that nearly drowned out the sound of the wind blowing across the prairie, and all the other sounds it caused. The cat outside had stopped begging to come in. Almost the very moment I noticed it, Grandma said, "He must have gone under the house." How did she know what I was thinking? Or maybe, again, we were just thinking the same thing. Either way, what was happening was more than just silence; it was a oneness of soul and spirit and mind. And Grandma just sat there, relaxed, near the warm kitchen stove, her eyes closed, the palm of her right hand covering her right eye, her thumb on her cheekbone and her fingertips gently resting on her forehead, while her elbow rested on the palm of her left hand crossed in front of her.

Perhaps she was thinking about the unexpected and unknown visitors who suddenly came to her parents house one night after dark. Not unlike the unexpected and unknown visitor who had come to our house that evening. She was very young then. It was one of those times when she was home from boarding school for a short period. Her father had finished the log house and the family had moved into it from the tent in which they had been living until that time. "It was about nine o'clock at night," Grandma said, "when the dog began to bark. Just the way he was barking, my father could tell that there was something or somebody strange near the house. While the dog was still barking, and before he even had a chance to look outside," she said, "there was a knock on the door. Opening the door, he saw a man standing there. He was wearing a big hat and boots and had a six-shooter strapped to his waist. Behind him, a short distance from the house, stood three other men dressed similar to him, and four horses. He said, 'Old man, we are looking for a place to stay for the night. We would like something to eat. If you and your wife would be kind enough to help us, we would appreciate it and will pay you well. If it's going to be too much trouble, just say so and we'll keep going.'"

Grandma continued, "My father looked at my mother, then he said, with his very limited English, that they could stay. While the first man came into the house the other three unsaddled the horses and tied them behind the house. When the man saw my parents had a child, he told them to tell her not to be afraid." Grandma said, "Along with the harshness of his voice, there was also a kindness. Maybe my father sensed that when he gave his consent for them to stay with them for the night. The other three men didn't come in for a long while. When my father looked for them, they were sitting on the ground in front of the house. When he invited them in, they seemed to be glad. While this was going on, my mother was fixing them a meal. One of the other three men carried a cloth bag which was nearly full of coffee. He gave it to my mother, and seeing the big coffee pot near the fireplace, he asked if she would make a big pot of coffee. They all removed their hats and laid them on the floor, by the door. The last three men to come in also took off their guns and laid them near the door. The first man, however, unbuckled his gun belt and hung it on the back of the chair where he was sitting."

"My father didn't seem to think they were dangerous, as he tried to carry on a conversation with them as best as he could," Grandma continued her story. "My mother fixed them a meal, which they all seemed to enjoy. After they finished eating, three of them were going to smoke. They asked my father if he smoked. When he said, 'Yes,' they gave him a small bag of tobacco which he used in his pipe as he joined them. They told my folks all they wanted to do was to drink coffee and play cards throughout the night, and when it began to get daylight they would continue on their journey. The kind man even said I could go to bed if I wanted to because they wouldn't do anybody any harm. All three of us stayed up all night. My father even sat at the table and watched them play cards and drink coffee all night. I can still remember," Grandma said, "seeing a big ring on one man's hand. It looked like it had several diamonds in it."

"Early in the morning, just when it was starting to get daylight, they saddled their horses and left. Before they left, the kind man said if they came back this way again, they would stop to see them. They all said thank you to my folks. Then the first man gave my father a whole lot of dollar bills. I never knew how much they gave him, but my father said they paid him well. Those four men left," she explained, "but they never returned again." Grandma looked at me with a very relaxed smile on her face as she added, "We never did find out who they were."

Slowly standing up, rubbing the middle of her back with both hands, Grandma said, "Well, I guess it is time to go to sleep. The man with the airplane will be here tomorrow." That seemed to be on her mind. But it was a good thought: after tomorrow Grandma wouldn't have to skimp and save every crumb in the house. Maybe that is why she seemed so relaxed as she told her stories tonight. We were just about through another crisis.

Grandpa banked the fires, blew out the lights, and went to bed. There was the smell of burnt kerosene, the sound of the wind, the purring of the fire in the potbelly stove near my bed, and, a short while later, the sound of Grandpa snoring.

The next morning we were up early; a sense of anticipation filled the air. For breakfast we ate the last of the cornmeal and drank almost the last of the coffee. The wind was still blowing but not as strong as it had during the night. A light snow was falling as the sun faintly shone through. It gave a sparkle to the snowflakes as they rode the wind. The dogs began to bark. Looking out the window, we could see the yellow airplane parked close to the house. Somehow we had all missed seeing its approach and landing. The man from the Red Cross carried in a big box of groceries, too big to set on the table. He went back out to the airplane and took out another big box containing more food. Finally, with his last trip he carried in a fifty-pound bag of flour. Among the groceries, in addition to what was on the list, there was candy, tobacco, dry cereal, Jello, and canned soup, vegetables, and fruit. There was also meat, bread, and potatoes. It was like Grandpa and Grandma had been to town themselves! The man apologized for not being able to stay a little longer. Before he left, however, he said he would come back in a few weeks and bring several bags of coal for us, and he did.

Later we discovered that he took groceries to many Indian families and provided for them equally as well. We never knew who the man was or how he heard about us. After he brought the coal, we never saw him again. He was talked about, however, for a long time afterward.

Years later when Grandpa retold the story he didn't tell it exactly like it happened, but the meaning was there, and I guess that's what was important. It was a story that was told, and retold, about a heartwarming experience that happened in the middle of a long, cold, harsh winter. Knowing Grandpa and Grandma, they were grateful to this man for the rest of their lives—whoever he was.

8

It took Grandpa a while to regain his strength after his terrible nosebleed and hospitalization. From that time on, however, he began to sleep more and more during the day. Grandma continued to be her steady, reliable, and faithful self, even though her eyesight was deteriorating as the cataracts continued to grow. And as difficult as it was at times, we made it through the winter with enough food to eat and enough fuel to keep us warm, and, most important, no more major illnesses. In the spring the snow melted, filling the draws and ravines with crystal-clear cold water. Before we knew it, even though we had looked forward to it, the roads began to dry, the trees were budding, and the farmers were disking and plowing their fields in preparation for planting.

It was a wonderful time of the year. Perhaps the most freeing experience of the year came the day I no longer had to wear overshoes and a heavy winter coat to school. What also made this time of the year so happy and memorable was the preparation for Easter and Memorial Day. Those days were important and sacred links with our cultural heritage and poignant reminders of the meaning of life, in the present and the future.

It always began on some unexpected night while Grandma was sitting quietly before the kitchen stove, her right hand covering her forehead and her eyes closed. It was almost like she had thought something through until she couldn't keep from talking about it. She talked about her father and mother and her childhood life with them. Grandma was the only child of seven born to her parents who survived infancy. She use to say, "I was born in a tent and raised in a log house." The three of them lived about two miles from the Missouri River, close to the Nebraska line. Night after night Grandma would recall stories involving persons whom she knew and loved, events that had touched and influenced her life as a little child.

Grandma's father was named Phillip. He never knew his parents because while he was still a baby his father died and his mother abandoned him and ran away with a white man. During most of his early years he was bitter toward his mother. He even said, "If I ever find her, I will kill her." She never returned and he never found her.

Phillip was thus raised by his grandmother. He grew to be a very wise man. During his younger days he was a scout for the white soldiers. He was small in stature and his left hand was smaller than his right hand. He had only partial use of his left arm, as the result of an injury as a scout. That's why he was called Catka Ptecena, which means "Short Left Hand." Because of his relatively long contact with white soldiers, he learned how to speak a little English. Occasionally he would communicate with passing soldiers as they stopped at a trading post about five miles from where they lived.

One fall day while he was waiting at the trading post he heard about an old white woman who had been left behind by her family. They were fleeing from a band of Indians in Nebraska. Because this woman was old and sickly, they left her so they wouldn't be held up and maybe overcome by this particular group of Indians. Phillip hurried home to share this information with his wife. In the Dakota language he said, "I am going to find that old woman and bring her home. If she is left out there alone, she may be killed by those Indians or starve to death."

He hurriedly made his way south to the Missouri River, carrying an olive-green army blanket. Reaching the edge of the water, he tied the blanket around his shoulders, walked out into the water as far as he could, then began to swim until his feet could touch the bottom again. He managed to cross the river without getting the blanket wet. By this time darkness was falling.

Grandma, still holding her hand on her forehead, her eyes closed, continued, "He began to run. He ran downhill and walked uphill. It was getting darker and darker all the time. He could hear a wolf begin to howl, at a distance. He found the old woman." Grandma opened her eyes and gazed into space for a few moments, then said, "She was sitting under a tree, crying. When she saw my father she was afraid of him. He told her not to be afraid. He had come to save her. After he convinced her of this, he persuaded her to get on his back. When she did, he wrapped the blanket around her and his shoulders and tied two corners together in front of him. He began to walk back home with the old woman on his back. She began to cry and wanted to go back to the tree where he had found her. He took her back. There on the ground were her glasses, and tied to a tree limb was a leather bag with her medicine inside."

Grandma went back to her normal storytelling posture, with her eyes closed. She went on, "He walked and walked, carrying her on his back. When they got to the river again, he walked into the water. When he got into the deep part the old woman became afraid. My father said to her, 'Don't be afraid. Have you ever heard of a bear drowning?'" Grandma's father made it across the river and home with this old white woman, and they took care of her until spring, when she died. Grandma never knew her name.

Grandma talked about her mother, too. Her name was Nancy. She was a granddaughter of a Yankton Sioux chief by the name of War Eagle, who lived between the late 1700s and the middle 1800s. He was bilingual, and his role was similar to that of being the Secretary of State for his people. A monument in his honor stands high on the cliffs just west of Sioux City, Iowa.

Nancy did not go to school and spoke very little English. She could be described as an independent woman, a good cook, and a person with a keen sense of humor. Even though she did not know the language very well, there were times when she attempted to use English words, just to make people laugh. She was especially good at playing on words. Whenever the English word was similar to a Dakota word, she would use the Dakota word, which gave it an entirely different meaning. Instead of calling her husband to supper, she called him to "sapa," which means "black" in Dakota.

It was not unusual for Grandma's parents to go visiting at separate places at the same time. They did this even at night. One night Phillip and his daughter, Bessie, went to visit one family while Nancy went alone to visit another. She stayed until after dark. While on her way home she had to cross a bridge. As she approached the bridge she could see a man standing on it. She called to him to identify himself but got no response. After calling out several times she became afraid and started to back away. At that moment she heard the slapping sound of an old blind man hitting his pants leg with his cane, trying to get his bearings. He always walked the countryside alone. He could determine where he was by the sound of his cane against his leg. Nancy ran to where the blind man was and told him about the man standing on the bridge. He said he would go with her and protect her from whoever was there. The two of them walked toward the bridge, but when they got there, he was gone. They crossed the bridge together and the blind man escorted her home.

66

When she arrived home, Phillip and their daughter were already there. She told them about her experience, and after she calmed down they went to bed. During the early morning hours Nancy had a dream: she saw the man standing on the bridge again. This time he began walking toward her. She told him not to come any closer, but he continued to walk in her direction. She became so afraid that she began to cry and call for help. Almost immediately she was awakened by her own cry and her husband trying to wake her. While dreaming she had become so frightened that she had had a stroke. When she was fully awake, she discovered that her face was twisted to the side and she found it difficult to speak. In time she recovered almost completely and lived nearly twenty years more.

Those were the kinds of stories that Grandma shared, and came near reliving, as she sat in front of the cookstove night after night with her eyes closed, resting her forehead in her right hand. Those events and experiences which she reclaimed in my presence held my undivided attention. They stirred my imagination and helped me connect with my ancestors to the extent there were times when I felt like I too had known them.

In the mid 1800s the federal government had encouraged the Christian churches to develop missionary programs on the Indian reservations. Christianizing the Indian people would be a way of "civilizing" and Americanizing them, so the theory went. To proceed with this, and to prevent competitiveness, various religious groups were assigned jurisdiction over particular reservations and were provided with funding, by the government, to build schools and churches. This is why certain Christian denominations have had a long presence on various reservations. This is why, for example, Grandma's parents were exposed to the Episcopal church and the Presbyterian church.

For the most part, Grandma's parents attended the Episcopal

church not far from where they lived. Grandma's mother even had two cousins who were interested in becoming priests, and who went "out east" for several years to acquire an education. On returning, they told the Episcopal priest that they wanted to become priests, but he replied in no uncertain terms that Indians were "not good enough to be priests." Soon after that, Grandma's mother and all of her family left the Episcopal church and went to the Presbyterian church, known as the "Hill Church," because it stands on a hill and can be seen for miles around. Both Grandma and her father remained loyal to the Episcopal church in spite of this.

Grandma's father died in 1904, when she was twenty-seven years old, and her mother died about six years later. He was buried in the Episcopal cemetery on a hill overlooking the Missouri River. The old white woman whom he had rescued was also buried there, and so was Grandpa and Grandma's one-year-old son. Grandma's mother and her family were buried in the cemetery behind the Presbyterian church, along with the two cousins who were denied the opportunity to become priests. (There were other family graves whose location we never knew, like the burial places of Grandma's brothers and sisters who died before she was born.) So every Easter we visited and decorated the graves in the Episcopal cemetery, and on Memorial Day we did the same at the Presbyterian cemetery.

About a week before these special days, Grandma and Grandpa made arrangements to get to the cemeteries to clean the graves. Sometimes someone with an automobile took them and helped them do what needed to be done. Since there were no caretakers at the cemeteries and they had no lawnmowers, all the grass and weeds were removed with hoes, shovels, and rakes. Each grave was scraped clean, to the ground, and left without a blade of grass on it. The men usually did the hoeing, while the women raked the weeds and grass into a pile and the children carried it outside the cemetery. Sometimes, if the weather was right and the grass was not too dry, the weeds were raked into a pile along the fence and burned. It was at least half a day's work.

One time another Indian couple, Dan and Maggie Jandreau, took us with a team of horses and a wagon. It was so much more fun than going in a car. Both Grandma and Maggie packed food for our lunch, knowing we would be gone nearly all day. It took several hours to get to the cemetery. About halfway through the task of cleaning the graves, we paused for lunch.

Grandma and Maggie served no light lunch. They spread several blankets on the ground and set places for everyone. There was chicken soup and fried chicken, along with potato salad, fried bread, pie, cake, and coffee. The food was delicious and plentiful. For some reason it always tasted better when it was served and eaten outside. It was fascinating to listen to the older people talk about when they were young, how things used to be. Their conversations were interesting and humorous as the men talked about their early farming days and hunting experiences. When a group of older people got together to visit, the children were allowed to participate only by listening and by laughing when it was appropriate. To the grownups, silence was a sign of self-discipline and obedience.

After the meal we continued to clean the graves of our family members. When the work was completed and we were ready to start the long journey home, the women began to cry. It was almost like a ritual. The cry was unlike any I have heard anyplace else—more like chanting. They uttered words in Dakota as if they were talking to their loved ones while they were crying, telling them they still missed them and wished they could see them. While they were doing this, the men stood very quietly with their heads reverently bowed. It was a moving and mystical experience, going back to the Ghost Dance, in which one could almost feel the presence of the spirits of the deceased.

The day before Easter or Memorial Day, Grandma filled large bowls with fruit, candy, gum, and cigarettes or cigarette papers and tobacco, which she had purchased the last time they were in town. Next she took large handkerchiefs, of various colors and designs, and tied one around each bowl. When she was finished she had about two bowls for each grave. In addition, Grandma had asked one of Uncle Jim's stepdaughters to make flowers for each grave. They were red, white, and yellow crepe paper roses. She did all of this almost in a form of a sacred ritual.

The flowers and bowls were placed on the graves the morning of the special day. The flowers were left on the graves; the bowls, however, were given away, usually to someone who resembled the deceased loved one in some way—sex, age, looks, or behavior. Grandma said to one elderly man, "That grave over there," pointing, "is my father's grave. Take one of the bowls on it." He thanked her, then went to the grave and took one of the bowls. This was done in a very respectful manner and was considered an honor for the recipient. To another man, in his early thirties, she said, "My son is buried over there. You can have one of the bowls on his grave." It was a warm and gracious way of Christianizing the tradition of giving in honor of the deceased.

Yes, spring was a time when we got in touch with the past and reclaimed our roots. And year after year I discovered a new dimension of myself as I was taught to have respect for all the significant persons in my past. It was an opportunity for spiritual growth; a deeper understanding of where I came from, who I am, and to whom I belong.

9

There were times when it was not easy to know just how old Grandma had been during those unique childhood experiences of hers. While age is something of which most elderly persons in the Sioux culture are proud and not ashamed, her age at the time of each event she shared did not seem very important. "When I was about . . . ," she would say. Or "When I was between the ages . . . ," then she would go on with the story. Everything always seemed to fall into place. A story here and another one there; like a puzzle being put together, again and again, until one could see a whole panorama. Some of it was painted with the brilliance of awe and mystery, while other parts were tinted with tragedy and cruelty. Yet in the midst of the most poignant episodes there was a mood of celebration. Grandma was always celebrating her past, the present, and I suppose the future: her life.

Like many American Indians of her generation, she had gone to a boarding school. The one she attended was an Episcopal boarding school located in a little South Dakota community named Springfield. It was called Hope School, and was for both boys and girls. Later, during the following generation, the name was changed to Saint Mary's School and attendance was restricted to Indian girls. Although the school was coed at the time Grandma went there, the boys were very seldom allowed to play with the girls. A high fence was built down the middle of the playground to keep the two groups separated. At no time were boys and girls allowed to speak to one another through the fence. If a boy wanted to speak to a girl, he would have to go to the principal's office and make this request. Then the principal would send for the girl, and the two of them would have to visit there in the presence of the principal, even if they were relatives.

Grandma attended Hope School for a total of ten years. During that ten years she completed six years of schooling. "I missed my parents, so much," she said. "I never knew when my father was going to come to visit me. When he did, sometimes I would go back home with him. I would cry until he would tell the principal that he was going to take me home. There were times," she continued, "when I went home and stayed for about a week, then other times I did not go back until the beginning of the next year. Even then, I didn't want to go back to school, but my father made me go."

Grandma's memories of her school days were not the most nostalgic. She continued her education, and kept going back, apparently because that was her father's wish. The stories she told were filled with mixed emotions. Some of the events, as she related them, had a humorous side, almost hilarious, but she nearly always got into trouble while in school because she laughed too much or laughed at the wrong time.

"The food was awful," Grandma would say. "Most of the time it was not fit for anyone to eat. There was a big white woman who was in charge of the kitchen. She was not a very clean person, and sometimes mixed different foods together that nobody had ever heard of doing before. One day," she continued, "when it was my turn to work in the kitchen, this woman told me to put all the leftover food from the day before into a big pan and mix them all together. At first I laughed because I didn't think she was serious. She sort of got upset with me, and again told me to mix all that food together. So I did it. As I mixed it," Grandma said, "it looked so awful. I just couldn't help myself; as I stirred it, I said out loud, 'Here, piggy, piggy. Here, piggy, piggy.' I got in trouble for doing that and had to stand in the corner for the rest of the day and go without supper."

In addition, the students were punished for talking in their own native language. Sometimes they were whipped for it. "Of course we were all punished for that many times," she explained. "We would forget. It was so much easier and more natural to talk Indian. This happened not only in our school," Grandma said, "it was done in all the boarding schools."

Another common occurrence in boarding schools in the late 1800s and early 1900s was the changing of names. Grandma and her parents didn't have to deal with this issue because only the boys' names were changed. They were changed from their traditional American Indian names to European-type names. For example, when my paternal grandfather went to this same boarding school his name was changed from David Iron Eye to David Dudley. It was a cooperative effort between the church and the government to Americanize the native people.

Still another problem Grandma had to struggle with while in school was that of being left-handed. "They tried to change that, too," she said. "Every time I was caught writing with my left hand I was punished. One time, in the fall of the year," she went on, "the teacher caught me doing it again, so she tied my left hand behind my back for the rest of the day. That was the day that my father showed up to visit. When he walked in the first thing he noticed was my hand tied behind me. He became very angry. With his very broken English he asked why I was being treated like that. He said, 'She is no animal. Get her things. I am going to take her away from this place.' So they got my things and I went home that same day."

"I was about thirteen years old then," she continued, "and my father used to visit with me a lot, especially when we were going somewhere alone. This time as we traveled toward home in the wagon he didn't say very much; he was very quiet. He even had a stern look on his face. I could tell he was troubled about something else. He was still upset with the people at the school. But I began to wonder," she said, "why he came to visit when I had just come back to school about a month before. Then I realized there was something more that was bothering him. So I began to talk with him. I asked him what was wrong. I thought maybe something was wrong with my mother. But he answered, 'There are some bad things that are happening out west. I went to the store yesterday, and while I was there, the soldiers stopped. They were on their way to Pine Ridge.' He went on to say, 'I overheard them talking to the storekeeper. They told him there was trouble out west because the Indians refused to stop doing the Ghost Dance. And since we are getting ready to do the Dance of the Ghosts,' he said, 'there might be trouble on this side of the river, too.'"

Grandma paused for a few moments, then she continued, "My father looked at me for the first time since we started talking and said, 'That's why I came to get you. If there is trouble, I wanted you at home where I can be sure you are protected.' This was on Wednesday," she explained. "It took us nearly all night to get home. After it got dark my father made me crawl in the back of the wagon and go to sleep while we traveled the rest of the way." With a slight smile on her face, Grandma said, "When we got home, my mother was so glad to see us." But before Grandma

74

finished her sentence the expression on her face changed; the smile disappeared and was replaced by a frown.

She shifted her body slightly in her chair and gently rubbed her forehead and her right cheek, as she normally did when the mood of her stories was about to change or intensify. Her voice dropped, both in tone and in volume. "The next morning," Grandma continued, "as soon as we got up, my mother told us that someone had come by the day before and said they were going to have a Ghost Dance on Friday and Saturday. My father replied, 'Get ready today and we will leave in the morning.' Whenever he said, 'Get ready,' he meant we were going to stay for the whole doings. All during that day," she said, "my mother packed some food and dishes, along with bedding, while my father put fresh hay in the back of the wagon and made sure the tent was in good condition and he had enough stakes for it."

"Early the next morning, when I woke up, I smelled coffee and could hear my mother getting breakfast. My father was outside hitching up the horses to the wagon and was already loading things into the back of the wagon. A little while later he came into the house and we sat down to eat our breakfast." For just a brief moment Grandma moved her hand away from her forehead and looked in my direction.

Closing her eyes and placing her hand on her forehead again, she continued, "While we were eating, I asked my father to explain the Dance of the Ghosts. He said some of the Indians west of the river had a vision, and in it they were told to do the Ghost Dance and in the spring the white man will disappear, those who have been killed in battle with the soldiers will come back alive, and the buffalo will return. He told me all the Indians were doing the Dance of the Ghosts, including many widows whose husbands had been killed by the white soldiers. He said, 'This is a dance of peace, and as long as the Indians continue to dance they

75

will not do any more fighting. They will wait for the promised new earth.'"

After they finished eating their breakfast, Grandma and her parents loaded the rest of their supplies in the back of the wagon and began the long ride to the village of Greenwood to participate in the Dance of the Ghosts. Greenwood was about ten miles west of where they lived. It was a winding road on which they traveled, just a dirt road that consisted of two tracks. It followed along the bottom of the cliffs that were once the very banks of the Missouri River. Grandma sat in the back of the wagon, in the soft hay, looking back and viewing the scenery and tracks where they had been. At times she could see the river for miles downstream. It sparkled like glass from the sun. In some places the river flowed close to the road and other places it was at least a mile away. Soon the rugged cliffs began to smoothen out and become rolling hills, which meant they were nearing Greenwood.

"Looking toward the north," Grandma said, "we could see two more wagons being pulled by horses coming down the big hill, and still another wagon was about a mile behind us. Other Indians were traveling by foot. Looking up ahead, all we could see were wagons with horses tied to them, and tipis and tents set up in a big circle on the river bank a little ways behind the agency. We could see streams of smoke flowing into the air at several different places in the circle. And from the scent that was being carried in our direction by the northwest wind," she said, "we knew others had arrived early and started cooking. When we approached the outer edge of the circle we could see that there was no empty place within the circle to put our tent. So we started an outer circle, and as others arrived they continued to add on to it, until there were two large circles of campers, wagons, and horses."

Without pausing in the least, Grandma continued, "Before we

even began to unload the wagon, some of my mother's cousins came to our wagon and invited us to eat with them. They had a big kettle of soup, some biscuits, and coffee." Just the way Grandma described that meal, it sounded inviting and delicious.

"After we finished eating and visiting, the first thing my father did was remove the harnesses from the horses and lead them down to the river to water them. While he was doing this, my mother and I began to unload the wagon. About the time we finished unloading, my father brought the team of horses back from the river and tied them to the rear wheel of the wagon where they could get to the hay that was in the back of the wagon. Next," she continued, "we put up the tent and spread some hay in the area of the tent where we were going to sleep. Then my mother and I unrolled our bedding on top of the straw."

"When everything was all set up, my mother started a fire and began preparing our supper. Meanwhile," she said, "my father and I walked around, visiting with different ones camped in the two circles surrounding the dance ground. As we were walking, I noticed a large tipi that had been put up a little ways in toward the center of the dance area. It seemed different from the rest in the camp area; this didn't seem to have anyone camping in it. So I asked my father what that tipi was for." Grandma looked across the table at me once more, then went on, "He explained that the spirit of the dead would return to that tipi and enter the world again through the opening of the tipi. 'That's why they put that there,' he said." Grandma's voice got real quiet, then she continued, "When I realized what was going to happen, I began to get scared. But I didn't say anything to either one of my parents."

"As evening drew near, people began to gather around the dance area. I saw a group of men carrying a large drum toward a particular place along the edge of the dancing grounds. I could see some of the dancers walking around with their costumes on. I

77

could feel my heart beginning to pound faster. Then one of the older men made his way toward the center of the ring to make an announcement. He announced that there would be no Ghost Dance until tomorrow evening. Then he led everyone in prayer. Just knowing that there would be no Ghost Dance until the next night was enough to cause my heartbeat to slow down. A big fire was built in the center of the dance area that lighted almost the whole arena." With a smile on her face Grandma said, "I heard the drumbeat, then the singers began and almost everyone began to dance. And they continued to dance until the early hours of the morning. After several hours of watching them dance, my mother took me back to our tent and made me go to bed. I laid there," she said, "listening to the drum and the singers until I fell asleep."

There were a few seconds of silence, as though in that very moment Grandma was resting up for that which she was about to experience again through the vivid memories of her past. Before she continued, she took a deep breath and rubbed both of her arms at the same time, then went back into her usual and familiar position with her left arm across her front, her right elbow resting in the palm of her left hand, and her right hand partially covering her right eye and her forehead. All settled, she was ready to go on with her story. "The next morning everyone was up preparing their breakfast. Some of them prepared their own meals, while others joined other members of their family or friends for meals. My parents and I ate alone." There was a brief pause in her speech while her voice dropped and came to a sudden stop. It was almost as if for just a moment she wondered why she and her parents didn't eat with others.

"When we finished our breakfast," she went on, "my father and I watered the horses and pushed some hay over to where they could reach it. While we were doing this, my mother heated some water and washed dishes. The day seemed to go by so fast, I was so busy watching and listening to people that I nearly forgot to be afraid any more. In the middle of the afternoon, almost without me being aware of it, the drum was playing, the singers were singing, and most of the people were dancing."

"Suddenly," she said, "those who were not dancing began to look toward the agency. There was the agent, and two policemen, coming toward the dance area. I heard my father say to my mother, 'Here comes trouble.' We watched them as they walked over to where the singers were seated around the drum, singing. We could see the agent say something to them, but they continued to sing. So he and the two policemen stood there and waited. Before they stopped singing, two older men came over to where they were standing and began to talk with them. As they talked, everyone continued to sing and dance. We didn't know what they said to each other, but in a few minutes the three of them turned and went back to the agency. We didn't see them again for the rest of the day."

With only a slight hesitation she resumed the story. "The dance continued throughout the afternoon and into the evening. They didn't even stop to eat. Of course, that was part of the sacrifice that the dancers were expected to make in order to be a part of the Ghost Dance. My mother didn't take time to fix any supper. When I got hungry, she gave me some wateca (leftover food). My father didn't eat either; he just sat in the crowd, watching. In between songs and dances after it got dark, some of the men built another big fire in the center of the circle. The dance went on. At a certain time the dancing stopped and some women brought some food out into the dance area and placed it on a blanket in front of the empty tipi." Grandma looked at me again and with a smile on her face and a small chuckle she said, "For some reason I knew what they were getting ready to do, but I wasn't scared any more.

The fire had died down until it gave out just a small red glow. The air was chilly, with the crispness of a fall night. The sky was clear and the moon was nearly full. The drumming and singing stopped. Everything and everybody was quiet. There were no sounds—no owls, no children playing or crying, not even the sound of the wind."

Grandma removed her hand from her forehead. Still resting her elbow in her left hand, she pointed all four fingers straight in front of her and began to move them up and down slightly with the rhythm of the drum. Looking straight ahead, she said, "The drum began again, but this time they were singing a different song. The dancers began to dance with a different spirit. As they sang and danced, some of the women sitting on the edge of the dance area began to chant and sing along with the singers. All of a sudden the drum, the singers, and all the dancers stopped, all at the same time. Everything was perfectly still."

Grandma sat for a moment, also perfectly still. Then she slowly put her hand out and pointed straight ahead. "We could hear a big whirlwind in the west," she said, "and it was coming in our direction. Some of the people seemed to get scared. They began to back away. Some of them went back to their tents and wagons. But the dancers stood still, watching the empty tipi and listening to the whirlwind as it came closer and closer. I was sitting between my father and mother. I took hold of my father's arm. He looked down at me with a comforting smile on his face, then turned his face toward the empty tipi. The wind was coming closer and getting stronger each minute."

Grandma's voice was getting louder as she talked on. "When the whirlwind got directly behind the empty tipi," she said, swinging her hand in a backward motion, "all of a sudden the flap on the front tipi swung wide open!" She paused for nearly a minute, with only a slight smile on her face. Then she continued, "Next, the whirlwind turned to the north and went up the hill.

No one moved or made a sound until the wind was gone. Almost everything was still again. All we could hear was an owl up in the hills somewhere." Grandma was completely quiet again. "Then they began to sing and dance. Nobody discussed what had happened. They all seemed to know. There was a good feeling in the air for the rest of the night."

The next morning Grandma and her mother loaded the wagon while her father watered the horses and hitched them to the wagon. They, like everyone else, began their long journey home with a feeling of peace and calmness in their souls, but they had heard the owl. It was the first and only time that Grandma ever saw the Dance of the Ghosts. And she was very young at that. She added, "My father said to me, 'Never forget what you saw at the Ghost Dance, because you may never have a chance to see it again.' He was right," she said. "I never witnessed it again."

Grandma went home with her parents but did not return to school. From the time of the Ghost Dance until Thanksgiving it was only a few weeks. "My father decided that I should stay home the rest of the year," she said, "which was very unusual for him to do. He kept saying, 'Something bad might happen.'"

"Christmas came and we went to the Hill Church as we usually did. That night the minister prayed for the Indians out west. That was where the war was, where all the fighting took place, because that is where the Black Hills are located, with all the gold. Just a few days before, we had heard that Chief Sitting Bull had been killed. Everyone seemed to carry a heavy burden and great concern for everyone out there. Sure enough," she said, "four days after Christmas many Indian men, women, and children were massacred at Wounded Knee." Grandma covered almost her entire face with her right hand. Very softly she whispered, "They were all killed." She didn't say any more. Grandma was silent for the rest of the night.

Some experiences limit our trust in humanity, while other experiences transcend all time and events. Grandma's stories were like the latter, saddened by the memories of tragic and cruel inhumanity, and yet comforted and encouraged by the belief in the mystery of life, both here and beyond. It's like the voice of an owl sounding in the midst of a great whirlwind. It didn't matter how old Grandma was, it was the truth in her words that gave reason for celebration.

10

For Grandma and Grandpa, and most American Indians in Sioux country, illness and death is a universal experience with universal meaning attached to it. That is why some of the older American Indians and some who are not so old go to the medicine man during times of illness. They go there for physical healing and restoration to personal wholeness. They view illness as a time when they are out of step with the universe. At the same time, death is the experience that frees our souls, which continue to live and grow, the boundaries being no less than the universe.

Grandma found meaning in her relationships with other persons her age, especially the women in the church. Some of them had known each other since the first grade in boarding school. They had much to reminisce about, using the Dakota language. They shared a closeness that transcended time and day-to-day experiences.

Her major concern, however, was for the younger people of our race and culture. She knew that the next generation and those following would have to struggle with problems that were similar to and yet so unlike those with which her generation had had to deal. She feared what the use of alcohol would soon do to the image and self-image of our people. Being aware of their lack of interest in and unwillingness to learn the Dakota language, she believed that in the future, our people would lose an important part of their identity. With the language gone, so would be many of the stories with their unique richness and flavor this language imparts. The intense and empathetic Dakota words for which there are no equals in the English language would not be there for the people to comfort and support one another with during times of illness and death.

This could very well be the reason why Grandma always made it a high priority of her life to visit the sick and to care for the dying, especially when it was a younger person. It could also be that her grief over the sickness and death of a younger person had something to do with her grief over the loss of her infant son, who would have been one of the younger persons if he had lived.

It was rumored throughout the Indian community that Clement Good Teacher's health was failing. The rumor must have been true, since Grandma was overheard praying for him several times. She seemed to sense something serious and urgent about his condition.

Clement was in his late twenties. His wife, Sarah, was somewhat older than he. I didn't know how long they had been married; they had no children. Clement was one of the few young persons his age who didn't go to school and did not learn the English language. He was a very skillful hunter and sometimes earned an income as a guide for other hunters during the hunting season.

One afternoon in the latter part of May 1949, Grandma announced that the next day she was going to visit Clement Good Teacher, as she often said, "before it is too late." Grandpa simply looked at her and said, "He must be getting pretty bad off." Grandma answered, "That's what they say."

Early the next morning Grandma was up and working in the old kitchen. She prepared some vegetable soup, baked a cake, and wrapped a relatively fresh loaf of bread in a dish towel, to take with her on her visit. She asked me if I wanted to go with her, to which I answered, "Yes." By midmorning she was ready to go. We went through the same routine of bringing the dogs into the house so they wouldn't follow us. This time it worked, and none of the dogs, not even Alex, tagged along.

Instead of going westward, up the hill toward the church, we followed the road that went north, over the big hill and past the one-room school which I attended and which had just recently recessed for the summer. Clement and his wife lived about a quarter of a mile north of the school, in a one-room house. Crossing the bridge to the other side of the creek, we followed the road up a little hill and went north along the creek. Their house sat out in the middle of a hay field. When we arrived, Sarah and two other women were there. Having seen us coming across the field, Sarah greeted us at the front door. Because this was a traditional family, Grandma immediately began to speak in the Dakota language and continued to do so all the while we were there.

Grandma handed Sarah all the food she had brought. Sarah thanked Grandma and placed it on the table and the stove. She knew what it was for and exactly what to do with it.

Very slowly and quietly Grandma made her way to Clement's bed, but not before shaking hands with the other two women who were present. Standing beside Clement's bed, she gently placed her hand on his forehead. He briefly opened his eyes, then closed them again. He was too weak to shake her hand, which was the appropriate thing to do. Because he was too ill to show Grandma this respect, she touched him on his forehead again and softly said, "Tehika, onśidaka ce." In a very weak voice he

Top left:
*Phillip (left back), Dorothy, David
(right), and me (left front) visiting at our
father's house in Yankton in 1946. Dorothy is holding a half-brother who didn't
live with us and whom we never got to
know.*

Bottom left:
*Grandma and Grandpa on the porch of
our old house on Choteau Creek in the
spring of 1956.*

Above:
*Two years after I joined the air force I was
stationed at Laredo, Texas.*

answered, "Hau." Those are words that are almost impossible to translate into English. They simply express an awareness of how difficult and humbling one's situation must be. And he affirmed it.

A chair was brought for Grandma to sit on. She sat beside Clement's bed, facing him, with her hands in her lap. She just sat there for a long while, in complete silence. Every so often he would open his eyes and say something, to which Grandma would respond in a very supportive way.

Grandma was not the only person who sat in a meditative silence. Everyone in the room joined her by being still, looking down at the floor, or sitting with their eyes closed. This continued until a spirit of oneness was felt, and the strength that came with this oneness. I was reminded of the words of the Psalmist: "Be still and know that I am God."

After what seemed a long period of silence, Sarah began some activity in the kitchen area. She was dishing out the food that Grandma and I had brought with us. Placing a small bowl of soup and half a slice of bread on the stand beside his bed, Sarah gently awakened Clement and explained that Grandma had brought some food for him. She asked him if he was ready to taste it. He answered, "Hau." Sarah raised his head and placed another pillow under it. He opened his eyes and managed to keep them open. She laid a hand towel on his chest and under his chin. Very carefully she gave him the first teaspoonful of soup, just clear broth. He managed to swallow it and keep it down. Sarah asked him if he wanted some bread. His answer was "Hau," but he wanted it soaked in the soup. The second spoonful consisted of a small piece of bread and broth. Again he managed to swallow it. The third spoonful was only soup. That was all he could handle gracefully.

Looking at Grandma, he said, "Yupiya. Nina pidamaya." ("Tastes good. Thank you very much.") Then he was ready to lie back down. The extra pillow was removed from under his head and he returned to his original position. He was exhausted, but he had managed to do what was expected of him; he had tasted Grandma's food, if only a tiny bit. In spite of his illness, he still was able to gather enough strength to show his respect and appreciation. It was exhausting just to watch this touching scene.

It was moving for Grandma, too. As Clement was attempting to eat, she sat relaxed but very still. At short intervals she quietly sighed and spoke a word of encouragement or empathy. The effect it was having on Grandma was evidenced by the moistness around her eyes. It was very apparent that she was struggling with him—that she was trying to help him struggle, not just for food, but for breath and life.

Sarah removed the dishes and the remaining food from the stand. She immediately transferred the food from Grandma's cake pan and kettle into her own containers. While she was busy doing this, Grandma continued to sit close to Clement, talking almost in a whisper. In between her sentences, without opening his eyes, he responded by saying, "Hau." When she was finished he said, "Hau, pidamaya." Grandma stood up, looked at him very intently, then turned and walked to where the other women were sitting. A brief friendly exchange took place, nothing important, just some small talk and a little bit of humor. Grandma picked up her belongings and handed them to me. She stood there by the kitchen table and began talking to them, speaking words of encouragement, faith, and hope. She spoke for about ten minutes before she walked over to Sarah, shook her hand, and whispered a special word of support. Then she was ready to go. This all happened, from beginning to end, in less than an hour. And it was obvious that Grandma's visit was appreciated by everyone.

A few minutes later we found ourselves on our way back home. Now that the cake pan and soup kettle were empty, they were much lighter to carry. By the sound of Grandma's heavy footsteps, however, it was apparent that the burden that she carried was very heavy. She continued to walk at a steady pace as we crossed the bridge, making our way toward the schoolhouse.

"Grandma," I said, "I'm thirsty. Can we stop for a drink of water?" "That would be nice," she answered.

The old pump had been standing on that well as long as I could remember. It was not very dependable during the summer. There were times when the leathers dried out and just would not suck the water up. It would have to be primed then.

Today we were going to try our luck. I began to pump. With only five pumps the water began to pour from the spout. First Grandma washed the opening of the spout with her hands. Cupping her hands together, she filled them and drank several handfuls of water. When she was finished, she pumped the handle a few times while I covered the spout with my right hand and, leaning over, drank directly from the spout. The water was cold and refreshing, just what I needed.

Instead of going on right away, we sat down, without saying a word to each other, on the steps of the school. The sun was still high, so there wasn't any shade there. But we sat and rested for a few moments. I think we were both emotionally drained. I sat there looking around at all the big trees along the creek. Grandma just looked down at the ground.

Then I broke the silence. "Grandma," I asked, "what did you say to Clement?" Without looking up she answered, "I asked him if his relatives have come back to see him. Then I asked him if he was ready to go with them." Without giving it a second thought, I went on, "Why did you ask him that?" "Because," she answered, "when someone is seriously ill and is going to die, their loved ones who have already died come to get them." She paused for a moment, then continued, "He said he was ready to go with them. That means he's ready to die."

90

Grandma stood up. It was clear that she was ready to go and did not want to talk about it any more. On our way home we talked about this and that; we even laughed about some things. All the while, though, there was the sound of her footsteps. The heaviness of her soul seemed to be weighing her down.

The next day while we were eating dinner, the dogs began to bark. Just by the way they barked we could tell that somebody was coming to the house. Grandpa looked at me and said, "Go see who's coming." Before I got to the door there was a knock. It was Tommy! I invited him in immediately. Coming into the middle room, where Grandpa and Grandma were finishing their dinner, he greeted them and they returned his greeting.

Grandpa asked him, "Have you had your dinner yet?" "No," he replied. "Find yourself a chair," Grandpa said, "and pull it up to the table." Without saying a word, Grandma got up to get Tommy a plate, cup, and some silverware. Then she poured him some coffee.

When she was seated again, Grandpa said, "Well, Tommy, what's the latest?" "Well," he said, then he paused, "I bring you bad news." I could see Grandma looking down, not with her head, but with her eyes. She seemed to know what he was going to say. "Clement Good Teacher died last night." He paused again, then went on, "The wake will be tonight and his funeral will be tomorrow." Nothing more was said about Clement or his death. Tommy stayed until late that evening, then went back home.

The next morning Grandma was up and busy in the kitchen. When she got up, she put on one of her good dresses and a fresh apron. I saw her good shoes, still in the box, sitting on the bed. After breakfast and the dishes were done, she sat on the edge of their bed, combing, braiding, and rolling her hair. Then she slipped on her good shoes and tied them securely. Taking out from her trunk the black beaded velvet bag with her hymnal and prayer book in it, she was ready to go to the funeral.

After the dogs were successfully brought into the house, Grandma took off her apron and out the door we went. This time one of the cats decided to follow us but was sidetracked before we got to the gate, which was only a few hundred yards from the house. We walked between the fields, across the dam, and on to the familiar trail that led up the hill toward the church. While we were still a distance from the church we could see the hearse was already there. We knew Clement's body was to lie at their small house, where the wake was, all through the night. Then it was to be brought to the church house, just west of the church, several hours before the funeral. That's the way it was always done, and that was why the hearse was there so early.

Instead of following the road, Grandma said, she wanted to go through the hay field and to the cemetery. We did this, in spite of the fact that it looked like it might start raining any minute. Clouds were gathering in the west. Some of them were dark clouds, and they were moving in our direction.

After making our way through the hay field, we crossed the ditch beside the road and walked along the fence that surrounded the cemetery, until we came to the main gate. Following the main road into the cemetery, Grandma said, "Look for the grave." Pointing to the west, she continued, "It should be on this side of the road."

After passing a few rows of graves, I spotted a pile of dirt to our left. "There it is, Grandma," I said. I showed her right where the grave had been dug. As we approached it we could see that the opening was covered with some planks. She walked up to it and looked it over very carefully. It was quite clear that she wanted to make sure the grave was completely covered. It had been covered to her satisfaction. Now she was ready to go up to the church house for the funeral.

On our way I asked her, "Why were you so concerned about the grave being covered real good?" "Because," she answered calmly, "it looks like it might rain, and if it rains or snows in an open grave, then someone who is close to the person for whom the grave was dug will also die, very soon. I wanted to make sure the rain wouldn't fall in it."

We hurried up to the church house, but it didn't rain. The storm clouds that had made Grandma go to the cemetery went to the north. The wind blew for a while and the temperature cooled off, but there was no rain.

The funeral was held in the church house because it was larger than the church itself. Even at that, not everyone who had come for the service was able to get into the building.

When the final hymn was sung, everyone passed by the shallow wooden cloth-covered casket that held Clement's body. It was a light blue-gray inexpensive casket. Grandma went before I did. I could see her from where I was sitting. I could see the sad look on her face as she paused beside the casket. With her right hand she touched his hand and said something, then went out the side door.

When it was my turn to walk by the casket, I did not pause, but continued to walk by very slowly. Clement looked so much like himself. He looked like he was just sleeping. He didn't even look dead. Questions came to my mind in that moment, questions that would have to wait until Grandma and I were on our way home.

When the hearse arrived at the cemetery with the casket in it, the casket had been closed and was draped with a star quilt. The casket was placed on the grave with the quilt blowing in what was now just a breeze. No one seemed to be in any hurry to start the committal service, since the weather had cleared and the sun was shining nicely again. Everyone waited until the minister was ready to begin.

Near the end of the service we sang the hymn "In the Sweet By-and-By" in the Dakota language. It had become a custom, a

tradition, to sing that song at the cemetery for almost every funeral. When we began to sing, four men stepped forward and
started lowering the casket into the grave with two long leather
straps. As they did this, Sarah and two other women began to cry
and chant as I had heard others do at funerals and other times at
the cemetery. I looked around to see if Grandma was crying too,
but she wasn't. She was standing back a ways, singing with that
sad look on her face.

Before I turned back toward the grave, I took a quick look at
everyone there. At that moment something mysterious caught
my attention. In the northwest corner of the cemetery, just outside the fence, was a big whirlwind. It was stirring up dust,
weeds, and leaves. There was something different about it; it
didn't appear to be moving in any particular direction. It just
stayed in one spot for what seemed like a long while, then it
moved on slowly.

I was so engrossed in the whirlwind that I almost forgot where
I was. Suddenly I heard someone pounding on wood. That's
when I realized where I was and what was going on. One of the
four men had climbed down into the grave and was nailing the
top onto the wooden roughbox. It was a harsh and disturbing
sound.

Gradually everyone passed by the family, shook hands with
them, and left the cemetery for the church house, where coffee
and lunch were being served. Grandma thought we should start
home rather than stay for the lunch. Without saying anything to
anybody we left. As Grandma said that day and every time we
started the long walk home, "Your Grandpa will be looking for
us."

Grandma again walked at a steady pace. This time, however,
her footsteps did not make that loud and heavy sound. In fact, I
could hardly hear them, even though she had on the same shoes
with the wide heels and was walking at a rather fast pace.

Grandma was in a hurry to get home and probably wouldn't take the time to stop and rest. If I was going to ask her any questions, I would have to do so while we were walking. Because the weeds were tall as we made our way down the hill toward the dam, we had to walk in single file. This was not very conducive to asking questions. They would have to wait until we were back on the road, beyond the dam. When we got there, we walked side by side.

I began my questioning: "Grandma, why did they have Clement's funeral so soon? And how come he didn't look dead? He looked like he was sleeping." Without the least hesitation she answered, "That's because he wasn't embalmed. When a person is embalmed, they look different and last longer. Since it is summer and he wasn't embalmed, his body would have started to spoil. That's why he was buried so soon."

That was a pretty simple answer, I thought. But I had a burning desire to tell Grandma about the whirlwind. So I began, "Grandma, while everyone was singing that last song at the cemetery, I saw a big whirlwind just outside the fence. It didn't move for a long while, then it went to the northeast. While I was watching it, I had this strange feeling come over me. What do you think it was?"

In her calm and peaceful way she said, "That must have been his relatives coming to take his spirit home with them." Before she was through answering my question, her expression showed that a great burden had been lifted. It was good to see her smile again. And I understood why, when a whirlwind went by, she always said, "Somebody died."

A few minutes later we were back home, and Grandma was right; Grandpa was looking for us. He was sitting in the old kitchen, looking out the door. When we walked in he said, "How was the funeral?" Grandma simply said, "Sad," then went into the other room to put away her hymnal and prayer book and to change her shoes. When she came back, she had on her clean apron and began preparing a meal for all of us.

Grandpa just sat there watching her. Then he spoke up, "Why do funerals have to take so long?" Grandma didn't react in the least, and neither did I. That may have been his way of saying, "I get so lonesome here alone."

In the coolness of that evening I sat, alone, in a patch of buffalo grass partway up the hill west of the house. The sky was full of devil's needles (as we called dragonflies) until the horizon darkened. Lightning bugs by the hundreds teased each other with their flashing lights. The world was full of mystery—whirlwinds and loved ones whom we call "dead" returning to accompany us on our way, just as in the Ghost Dance! Many questions spun around in my mind as a result of the last few days. But one thing was for certain: Grandma's burden had been lifted and the sadness in her face was gone. It was as if she tiptoed into a new day. I suppose it was because she knew that Clement was back in step with the universe, and to some degree so was she.

11

Saturday was the busiest day of the week, so it seemed. Regardless what time of the year it was, Grandma and Grandpa were up early in the morning. During the summer, however, they were up even earlier, since it got light so early. Saturday was when Grandma did her baking for Sunday, and the housecleaning, the washing, and sometimes the ironing were done. If there was no rain water left over from a previous rain, we hauled the wash water from the creek. Sometimes this was done on Friday night, but more often than not it was done early Saturday morning. It usually took four trips before we had enough water to do all that had been planned.

The last thing I would say to Grandpa the night before was "Grandpa, wake me up early in the morning," but seldom did he have to awaken me. Just knowing there was work to be done was enough to wake me earlier than usual.

Waking up, I heard only the muffled voices coming from the old kitchen. In the summertime the cookstove was moved back into the old kitchen and that is where Grandpa and Grandma sat and had their first cup of coffee. It was a pleasant old room with the front door opened onto the porch and the north window open. The kitchen was on the west side of the house, which made it much cooler with the morning breeze blowing through. When they were younger and in better health, Grandpa and Grandma sometime hauled all the water before I was awake. As time went on, however, and their health failed noticeably, that happened less and less.

I lay there for a few minutes, one morning, enjoying the peace and quietness. I could hear the tree leaves rustle in the gentle breeze. Wonderful songs were being sung by the birds; a meadowlark in the apple tree sang out above the rest. The sun shone freshly through the east window and the open door as it silently announced another new day.

For a moment I thought I heard Grandpa mention David and Dorothy. I lay very still, listening intently. Then he said it again. It was June already, and nearly six months since they had left. We hadn't heard from them and didn't know how they were. This played heavily on Grandpa and Grandma, although once I had adjusted to their absence I didn't think of them very often. Above all, I didn't worry about them. But they remained a major concern for Grandpa and Grandma. For sure, I heard Grandpa mention David's name. He must have had some insight about their welfare. Or again, maybe he just knew.

I got up, put on my clothes, and went out to the old kitchen. As soon as they heard my footsteps they stopped talking about David and Dorothy. After a "Good morning," I grabbed two galvanized pails and went down to the creek. The water was so clear and cool. I set the pails aside, knelt down on a large, flat rock, and leaned over to wash my face and hands in the running stream. It was such a good way to wake up. Then I dipped each pail into the stream and they were filled almost instantly. I hurried back to the house with the first two pails of water. By the time I got there, Grandma and Grandpa had set out the teakettle, a large blue porcelain canner, and a big galvanized washtub for me to pour the water into. I continued to haul water until Grandpa or Grandma told me that would be enough. The teakettle and the canner were immediately placed on the cookstove to heat. Then I discovered Grandma had prepared breakfast while I was busy hauling water. She always fixed a good breakfast: pancakes, eggs, bacon, and coffee.

By the time we finished eating, the water on the stove was hot. After clearing the dishes away, we began washing clothes. We took two straight-backed chairs and set them in the middle of the room, facing each other, and placed one of the big washtubs on the seats. Next, the washboard with the corrugated glass for rubbing was put into the tub. Grandpa and I carried the big blue canner full of hot water from the stove and poured it into the tub, adding more water to cool it down. Then we placed the other washtub on the stool and poured cool water into it for the rinse water. After adding powdered soap to the hot wash water, we were ready to start. When Grandpa was younger he did most of the washing, especially wringing out the heavy pieces. But now Grandma and I took turns. First we washed the white clothes, then the colored clothes, and last the overalls. After scrubbing an item on the washboard, we wrung it out by hand, then put it in the rinse water. Once all the white clothes were in the rinse water, they were wrung out again by hand and were hung out on the line to dry. We continued this until all the clothes had been washed, which wasn't very long because we didn't have many clothes.

When the washing was done, the wash water was poured out on the grass. The rinse water was saved and used to mop the floors that same day. I liked to mop the floors because it made them look like new for a while. The floors in the middle room and the room where we slept were covered with old linoleum. In some places most of the design was faded or had worn off. When the mop water was spread on it the colors darkened and the design stood out. I wished it would stay that way, but once it dried, it was the same old faded linoleum even though it was clean. Around the edges of the linoleum, where the wood floors showed, the wood was so old and dry that the water soaked into the floor almost faster than we could rinse and dry it.

When the clothes on the line were nearly dry, we placed the heavy flatirons on the cookstove to heat them. While the shirts were still a little damp, they were brought in and rolled in a towel to keep them from drying out completely and to even out the dampness. When the irons were hot we ironed the clothes that needed it. Grandma taught me as a very young boy how to iron my clothes with those heavy old irons. They were oval in shape, coming to a point on each end, with a hole in the top center where the handle attached. All three irons were heated on the cookstove while I was mopping. The wooden handle was shaped like a half circle and had a knob in the middle to attach it to the irons. Before an iron was used we moisten a finger and quickly touched the bottom of it. If it sizzled, the iron was ready. When an iron cooled it was set back on the stove and replaced with a hot one. But before a fresh iron was used, it was rubbed against a piece of waxed paper to make it slide more smoothly over the material.

An army blanket on the kitchen table served as an ironing board. I suppose every Indian family had an army blanket. They were tough, scratchy, tightly woven wool in an olive-brown color. They were warm in the winter and worked well for an ironing board cover. Usually while I was mopping, and ironing in the middle room, Grandma was in the old kitchen doing her baking. By the middle of the afternoon we had clean clothes, a clean house, and Grandma had her Sunday baking done.

It gave me a good feeling of accomplishment. Our goal was to finish before the temperature got too high, which we did most of the time. Grandma always tried to show her appreciation for all I did by baking something extra, which she served when the work was done. She made all sorts of good pies, for example. This time she made a lemon pie, which she cut for all of us to enjoy.

When it got real hot, in the middle of the afternoon, it was time for a cool drink of water or Kool-aid. About an eighth of a mile north of the house there was a spring where the water always ran cold. We got only our drinking water from there because it was not as easily accessible as the creek and because it was not a very forceful spring. It had been there for as long as I could remember. Every year when the snow melted, the water went gushing down through the draw and covered the spring with mud. So in the springtime we would go there and dig a hole where the water was standing and clear a way for it to flow into the creek. After making a hole so big and so deep, we could see the water beginning to bubble. Then we knew we were digging in the right spot.

We had two glass jugs that we used to carry the spring water to the house and store it in. They were both covered with burlap to keep the water cool longer. I took the two jugs and walked to the spring and very carefully filled them, using a big dipper, trying not to rile the water. When they were both full I put the covers on them, then dipped them into the spring to get the burlap wet and cold.

I hurried home so the water would still be ice cold when I got there. By the time I reached the house both of my pants legs were wet from the wet burlap wrapped around the jugs. Grandma and I laughed about it.

Grandma had the glass pitcher, a package of Kool-aid, and the sugar sitting on the table. I liked to open the package of Kool-aid and pour it into the pitcher and to smell the rich odor of the powder. That day it was orange. After adding the right amount of sugar, I immediately filled the pitcher with cold spring water. A light-orange-colored foam appeared on the top. As I stirred the Kool-aid with a big spoon it was fun to watch the sugar crystals go spinning around and around. Gradually the crystals disappeared and the drink was completely clear. I poured three glasses of ice-cold Kool-aid. I handed one to Grandma, who thanked me and said, "I'm going out to the east side of the house to sit in the shade for a while." By that time the sun was beginning to go down in the west. It was at this time of the day that Grandpa and Grandma sometimes sat outside in the shade. I took Grandpa's glass of Kool-aid to him in the other room, where he sat in his rocking chair listening to the radio. As usual he said, "Wait a minute," and he drank up his glassful in a few seconds. After breathing a sigh of enjoyment, he said, "Thank you," and handed the glass back to me.

Taking my glass, I went outside to sit with Grandma. She had taken an old quilt and spread it out on the grass and weeds that served as our lawn. When I sat down beside her, she asked, "Did you give your Grandpa his drink?" "Yes," I replied. Looking in my direction, she asked, "Did he drink it up already?" "Yup," I responded. At that she began to grumble, "He doesn't even take the time to enjoy it. He's afraid he might miss part of his ball game." Grandma was not much of a grumbler, but she always grumbled about the way Grandpa hurriedly drank what she considered a treat. She thought he should take his time and enjoy it. That was how she drank hers.

For me it was a treat just to sit outside with Grandma. All three dogs came around and lay down near us. Tizer rolled in the grass, making contented noises. The other two dogs seemed to be looking for something to get excited about. One of the cats sat beside Grandma while the other one looked for a big catch in the weeds not far away. It was like a family, a universal family. Grandma talked to the animals like she was talking to me or some other person. Sometimes it was hard to know who she was talking to.

Then she gazed into the east for a moment. I could sense by the look on her face and the tenseness of her body that she was making her way back in time, her time. She was thinking through some significant event in her life that she was about to share. Even the dogs seemed to sit up and take notice. Looking toward the eastern horizon, she began to speak with her unique storytelling diction and tone of voice.

"When I was a little girl," she said, "my folks and I went to the Hill Church on Christmas Eve. One Christmas Eve, after the worship service, everyone went outside of the church and stood around for a while. We were getting ready to go over to the church house to eat lunch and have the Christmas tree." By "have the Christmas tree" she meant they were going to exchange gifts and pass out the fruit, candy, peanuts, and so forth. "Everyone stood around visiting. All of a sudden," she said, "we could hear voices. It was the sound of a choir singing. Everyone got real still." Pointing toward the southeastern horizon, she went on, "There in the southeast corner was a bright light. Then we began to see people walking in the sky. They were wearing choir robes. They were singing, but we could not make out what they were singing. First there were men, then women, then children making a procession across the sky."

All the while she was describing this nearly indescribable scene, her hand moved slowly across the eastern horizon. Then, pausing in that direction, she exclaimed, "Then they disappeared in the northeastern sky, but we could hear them singing until the last child disappeared. Everyone was silent. Then the minister said, 'Let's all go back into the church and thank God for the privilege of seeing this because we probably won't ever see something like this again.' So we all went back in for a prayer of thanksgiving."

This was the first time I heard that story. Grandma told it several times afterward, and each time it was the same; nothing changed. This time it was almost like experiencing Christmas in

June. The mystery of the event had so permeated Grandma's life that when she told the story something holy and radiant could be felt. "As far as I know," she concluded, "that has never happened again."

We sat in silence for a while, which was not unusual. For when Grandma recalled something of her past, it usually was awesome and breathtaking. That day she led me back with her into that unforgettable Christmas, and it took me a while to return to the present and realize where I was.

I broke the silence by asking, "Grandma, would you like some more Kool-aid?" "Yes," she answered, "Is there any left?" "It might be warm by now," I said. To this she responded, so graciously, "That will be all right."

I quickly went into the old kitchen to pour each of us another glass of Kool-aid. Sure enough, it was warm, but there was almost enough to fill two glasses. As I came around the front of the house I saw someone walking toward the house. I saw him even before the dogs did. He was short, and wearing jeans and a white tee shirt. When he was halfway between the creek and the house I recognized who he was. It was David! I could hardly believe my eyes.

I used to wonder what would happen if he and Dorothy, or one of the two, came home. How would Grandpa, who was sometimes a stern and harsh person, react? I knew he was disappointed because they didn't return at the end of their Christmas vacation. I also knew he was upset with Dad for not returning them. I guess I always knew how Grandma would respond. She would be glad to see them and would welcome them home under any kind of circumstances. But Grandpa, he was different. What was he going to do and say?

I began to feel a bit of uneasiness coming over me. David must have been feeling something of the same as he came closer and closer. One of the dogs spotted him and suddenly began to bark, and the other two followed. Straining her eyes and looking in that direction, Grandma said, "Someone is coming." Knowing that she wouldn't be able to recognize him until he got very close, I said, "Yes, Grandma, it's David." With a smile on her face, her eyes misty, she looked at me and said, "Is it? Really?" She got up from her quilt as fast as she could. Staggering for a few steps, then more steady, she went to meet him. All I could hear her say was, "Well, hello! My poor boy." She put her arms around him and held him. They were far enough away that I couldn't hear much more than that, but I could see the movement of Grandma's body. I knew she was crying. Then I heard her say, "Come in."

At that point I went to greet him. It was not much of a greeting, for sure. Perhaps not what it could have been and should have been. We both had someone else on our mind—Grandpa. But we both laughed and hugged each other, each patting the other on the back.

After that we made our way into the house, Grandma first, then David, and then me. When we got into the old kitchen, Grandma turned and stepped aside to let David go first. Slowly he walked into the room where Grandpa was still sitting in his rocking chair. The whole house was in dead silence. David approached him and in a weak and trembling voice said, "Hello, Grandpa." Grandpa turned and looked to see who was there. Without the least hesitation he reached out for David and said, "Well, I'll be damn, here's our boy." And Grandpa hugged him and David began to cry.

A feeling permeated all four of our lives and transcended all that we were to expect during that time of the year. Grandma's Christmas story fell into place and began to make sense. For as Grandpa was hugging David, I experienced Christmas still lingering in that little old house, on a hot summer afternoon, on

Choteau Creek. The whole world, or at least our world, was filled with love. There was a knot in my throat. I looked at Grandma and she looked at me. We both had tears in our eyes but we smiled at each other.

Early that morning Grandpa must have sensed it. And all that day, unknown to us, we were not just busy. We were preparing for a homecoming.

12

There was always something new and different about Sundays. This particular morning I awakened to the sound of the meadowlark singing its song from the very top of the apple tree. There was also the sound of a bluejay teasing another bird down by the creek, but it was the meadowlark that caught my attention and started my day off on a joyful note. The morning sun beamed into the house through the east window and the open door. The dewdrops on the grass sparkled in brilliant hues of blue and silver. The house smelled clean and fresh as a mild scent of soap still hovered in the air. After having a bath the night before, Sunday morning was when I put on crisp clean clothes with straight and sharp creases in the legs of my jeans and in my shirt sleeves. I was careful not to bend my knees any more than necessary lest I ruin the creases.

There were faint voices in the old kitchen. The one I could hear the most and the clearest was David's. He was up and dressed before I even woke up. He was telling Grandpa and Grandma why he had run away from Dad's house. One day he had had a misunderstanding with Dad's wife while Dad was at work. When Dad came home that evening, he was told to whip David. When Dad refused to do it, there was a lot of conflict between him and his wife. Because David felt like he was the cause of the problem, he decided to run away and come back home. The day before he left he told Dorothy what he was planning to do, so at least someone knew where he had gone.

David didn't stay with Grandpa and Grandma very long. About four or five months later, on a Friday afternoon, Dad's wife and Aunt Lucy, Dad's older half-sister, came to the school and asked permission to take us to Yankton for the weekend. David went but I refused. Again, Dad had no intention of returning David and me after the weekend. David was there only a few days, however, when Dorothy and Dad's wife had a disagreement. The next day Dad bought two bus tickets to Sioux City, gave Dorothy five dollars, and sent them to be with Mom. Less than six months later we received a letter from Mom telling Grandma and Grandpa that David and Dorothy were with her but that she was having problems getting David to go to school. She asked us to come and get him. So one Saturday Grandma and I caught a ride to the nearest bus stop, went to Sioux City, and brought David back home with us the next day. This time David stayed with Grandma and Grandpa for the next four years. When he was fifteen years old, he once more went to be with Mom, who by this time had moved to Kansas City, Missouri. Although he returned to visit many times, he never came back to Choteau Creek to live in that old house again. Dorothy stayed with Mom in Sioux City and went to school there until she got married.

This morning I could hear Grandpa begin talking. Soon there was the sound of laughter! It sounded like a glad reunion taking place. Although I was anxious to put on my clean clothes, I stayed in bed for a while, not wanting to interrupt what was happening in the old kitchen.

Today was Sunday and that meant we were going to the small Episcopal mission church called Holy Name. When it rained on Sunday, it usually turned out to be a long, restless day. But the sun was shining and there was no rain in the forecast, which meant this would be a fun-filled, meaningful day.

Carefully putting on my clothes and slipping into my freshly polished shoes, I walked through the old kitchen with a quick greeting and hurried to the outside toilet. When I returned, Grandma was keen enough to notice that I had on the clothes I had freshly washed and ironed myself. She complimented me by saying, "You look nice today, all dressed up."

Breakfast was ready, so after I washed my hands and face and combed my hair, we all sat down to eat. As usual, I was the last one. Grandpa was waiting to say the grace. The conversation consisted mostly of talk about what had happened since David and Dorothy left: the winter storms, Grandpa's nosebleed, Tommy and me spearing fish, and the humorous things the animals did. When we finished eating, David and I washed the dishes while Grandma made a large bowl of potato salad. After the dishes were dried and put away and the table was wiped off, she went into the other room by herself. We all knew what she was getting ready to do. We three "men" stayed out in the old kitchen, talking and laughing.

About ten minutes later Grandpa said, "Well, we better go into the other room for prayers." We went into the room where Grandpa and Grandma and I slept. We found Grandma sitting on their bed, looking through her prayer book with her Bible lying beside her. Every Sunday morning, whether we went to church or not, we always had a short family worship service, which was led by Grandma. Because of her failing eyesight, she stood by the east window where there was plenty of light and always used a special prayer book that had rather large print. We each found a place to sit and remained very quiet.

When she was ready, Grandma stood up and read a lesson from the Bible. Then she asked us to stand and say the Apostles' Creed with her. Next we knelt to pray, all except Grandpa, who because of his bad knee used to sit in his rocking chair instead of kneeling. The prayers began with all of us saying the Lord's Prayer in unison. Then Grandma read a few of the prayers from the Book of Common Prayer. Those were followed by her extemporaneous prayers.

When Grandma knelt down, she faced her bed, her elbows on the bed, both hands covering her face. Her petition and thanksgiving came from deep within her. She prayed for Mom, all of us grandchildren, the sick, and those who mourn. She often asked God to send rain and "to feed and protect the wild animals and the birds of the air." Nearly every Sunday, just for a moment, I would open my eyes and glance at her. It always seemed like Grandma was in another world. And it was very clear she knew to whom she was talking. She ended the service with a benediction from the prayer book. We all remained kneeling in silence for at least a minute, or until we could hear her getting up.

Grandma's personal prayer was different each and every Sunday. The prayers that she read, however, were always the same. I had heard them a hundred times or more. I knew them by heart. This morning, when we finished the Lord's Prayer, I felt a touch on my left arm. Opening my eyes and turning, I saw Grandma with her hand on my arm and pushing her prayer book in front of me. She had never done this before. I took the book from her and very nervously began to read the prayers, one after another. At the end of each prayer everyone responded by saying "Amen." When I finished reading the selected prayers, Grandma proceeded with her own prayer and ended the service. It all happened so fast I didn't know what was going on. Without saying a word, Grandma put her prayer book and her Bible away and went back into the old kitchen.

By the time we got there, she had several dish towels out and was beginning to tie the food up in them. In one she tied two pies, one on top of the other. In another she wrapped and tied a cake, still in the cake pan. And in the third towel she tied up the large bowl of potato salad. Then she put together a bundle of cups, plates, bowls, and silverware. The last thing she did was to open her trunk quickly and get out her Dakota prayer book and hymnal, which she kept and carried in a black velvet bag with a beaded flower design on it. Now she was "all set to go," as Grandpa always said. Grandpa seldom went to church. One reason was because he couldn't walk that far, but mostly because he was not a church-goer. Only on special occasions did he go, like when David and I had our confirmation.

Before we left, Grandpa went out on the porch and called the dogs. His intention was to shut them in the house with him so they wouldn't follow us. Tizer, the little brown dog, and Ohitika (which means "Brave"), the older black dog, came running into the house. But Alex, the big, strong, white and black dog, went running up the hill and out of sight. He knew what was going on; this trick had been pulled on him before. All Grandpa said was, "He's pretty smart," and went back into the house. Grandma, however, was furious. She said, "He'll be walking around at church, bothering everybody." But Alex was gone and we were ready to start the long, two-mile walk to church.

When Grandma went to church she always wore her best. This morning she looked just beautiful. She had combed her hair early that morning, parting it across, from one side to the other, and made a small roll across the front. Then she braided the rest and rolled it into a bun in the back. She covered her hair with a navy-blue turban. Along with that she wore a dark-blue three-quarter-sleeve dress that hung below her knees. On her feet she wore her good black nursing-style shoes with a design on the toes. She topped everything off with her unique cross, which hung down her front on a blue and white beaded chain. It was the same kind of cross that Father Rouillard wore. It had been given to her when she was confirmed while still in the Episcopal boarding school nearly sixty years earlier.

Each one carrying some food, we began our journey through the gate, down the road between the two cornfields, across the dam, and up the hill toward the church. Alex kept his distance ahead of us. He knew where we were headed. David and I thought he was funny, but Grandma didn't.

This was the morning for meadowlarks. Almost all the way to the church we could hear them singing, sometimes very near, other times at a distance. Whichever, they all sang the same warbly song. This was also the time of the year for bluebells and wild roses to be in bloom. The bees, too, were out that Sunday morning, gathering all the nectar they could. To the smallest degree I could identify with them. It was not uncommon for me to go out on the hillside looking for bluebells that hadn't opened yet. When they were removed from the stem, they resembled little one-quart milk bottles. All I had to do was to suck on the tiny opening next to the stem to get a taste of the sweet nectar. This morning, however, we didn't have time to stop for that. Grandma was leading the way up the hill in the direction of the church.

When we reached the top of the hill, about half a mile from the church, we could hear the "first bell." It was just a reminder. On the days when we didn't go to church we could hear the bell all the way down to the house. It was a big black cast-iron bell that had a beautiful sound. It reminded me of what we were about to experience when the worship began. If we were still at home, the sound of the bell made me wish I had gone to church.

Only a few moments after the bell stopped ringing, we could see other people approaching the church. One family came all the way from down by the Missouri River using a team of horses. The man and his wife rode in the wagon with their two youngest sons, while the two older sons followed behind, riding their horses bareback. The father of this family made sure all the boys wore their best to church. So even on hot summer days they wore wool suits to church, which was all they had. To their father that was their best. The two older sons would walk into the church every Sunday with horse hair on the back of their pants and down their pants legs.

Some people who lived relatively close to the church walked to church just for the enjoyment while others drove their cars. Still others, like us, had to walk. Before we arrived at the church we could see someone walking to church from the south. The person walked very slowly. We could tell by the way she walked that it was Mrs. Ree. Most of the young people referred to her as "Grandma Ree."

Arriving at the church, we set our food on the table in the church house, along with that which others had brought. Almost immediately Grandma said, "Why don't you boys go and help Mrs. Ree?" "Okay," we said, and ran out the door and down the road to meet her. Mrs. Ellen Ree was a very heavy woman. She was round all over. She wore her hair in two long braids crossed in back and wrapped around the front of her head. On the very top of her head, surrounded by the braids was a navy-blue straw hat with a fine net that covered her forehead. Her skin was much lighter than Grandma's and her face was much rounder. Her nose and mouth were wide. She wore gold wire–rimmed glasses that were perfectly round. The legs and ankles of this lovely woman were two or three times larger than those of anyone else in the church. Her feet were big, wide, and fat. She wore black lace-up oxfords that looked like men's shoes. Once I overheard Grandma tell Grandpa that Mrs. Ree had dropsy. Today Grandma Ree had on a light purple dress which drew everyone's attention away from her imperfections, and in the center of her breast was her cross, just like Grandma's, shining like new on a black and white beaded chain. But her size didn't matter; she was a beautiful woman.

When we reached her, she was carrying two pies and a bowl of potato salad wrapped in dish towels in one hand and a big kettle of chicken soup in the other. In addition, she had her Dakota prayer book and hymnal in a brown beaded bag hanging on her shoulder. David took the kettle of soup and I took the pies and potato salad. She appreciated our help and told us what good boys we were. "Your Grandma has good grandchildren," she said. When she said this, she held the word "good" for a long while: "Gooood grandchildren." That was her way, and the Indian way, of saying we were very good.

It was time for the church service to begin. Everyone else was there. But we still had a ways to go yet and everybody knew it, so they waited. They wouldn't ring the "second bell" until we got there. And so we walked slowly with Grandma Ree.

Mr. Ree—Charlie was his name—didn't come to church very often. He was a tall and straight man who walked with a cane. He never said much. When he did talk, he did so in a soft-spoken voice and always used the Dakota language.

Several years before, one Sunday following the church service, Grandma and we three younger grandchildren went to visit Mr. and Mrs. Ree. This must have been prearranged, since only a short while after we got there Mrs. Ree served a big, delicious Sunday dinner. Charlie Ree did not come to the table to eat with the rest of us. They lived in a small house with two rooms, a kitchen and a bedroom. He stayed in the bedroom. Grandma Ree filled his plate and took it to him.

After we finished eating, the three of us kids went outside to play. The first thing, I noticed a long rope reaching from the corner of the house to the outside toilet. I had never seen something like that before and wondered why it was there. We had fun jumping over it. It was low enough so we could do so.

114

Then the old man walked out onto the small porch. He stood there, straight and tall with his head held high, as if he were looking over the hills before him. That was the first time I ever remember seeing Mr. Ree. He slowly stepped off the edge of the porch and walked with his right hand touching the side of the house. When he got to the corner he felt around until he got hold of the rope. He then followed the rope all the way to the toilet. I stood there, stunned. Charlie Ree was blind.

We went home and I never thought much more about Mr. Ree. A year or so later, one cloudy and windy day, all the men and boys were standing outside the church waiting for the church service to begin. Someone came walking down the hill to the south of the church. Whoever the person was, he or she was walking quite fast. We waited and continued to visit and practice our Indian humor (it was evident that some of us needed the practice). As the person came closer, we could see it was a man, a tall man, wearing a long black coat and walking with a cane. We watched him come closer and closer. Rather than follow the driveway, he went down into the ditch, back up again, and walked through the meadow. When he arrived at the church, I was amazed. It was Mr. Ree, walking straight and tall. And Charlie Ree could see. The words of an old hymn immediately came to my mind: "I once was blind, but now I see." It was a miracle! Later I learned that he had had cataracts removed from his eyes.

This Sunday Mr. Ree wasn't with Grandma Ree. She came to church alone. As we neared the church yard we could see the church surrounded by old cars. All of them were ten or fifteen years old. I liked every one of them. They were all shapes and sizes. There were two-doors and four-doors. Two of them were coupes with rumble seats. All the windshield wipers swung down from the top of the window. Some of the windshields even opened up from the bottom. Some of the wheels had lots of steel spokes, while others had large wooden spokes. But the cars all had large running boards and front fenders with big, round head-lights on them. For a pastime I sometimes walked around the church yard looking at all the cars, wondering what it would be like to own one of them.

While the "second bell" was ringing we went into the church. That Sunday the church was full. In fact, not everyone could get into the church, since the building had room for only about forty people. This happened, not every Sunday, but often. So the four stained-glass windows were opened at the bottom and the front door was left open. Those who stayed outside stood near one of the openings and listened.

The women and young children sat on the left side of the church while the men and older boys sat on the other side. Part of this had to do with being close and separate at the same time. In the Sioux culture, those who practiced the traditional ways, the son-in-law and mother-in-law never spoke to each other. Neither did they look at each other, and they avoided talking in a loud voice in the presence of the other. This was a sign of respect. They spoke to each other only during times of emergency, when no one else was around. Even then they were not supposed to look at each other. And if they both spoke and understood the language, they used Dakota to communicate. They spoke seriously, quietly, and briefly. By sitting separately, both groups were free to sing and worship in a loud manner if they chose to do so, uninhibited.

One of the most beautiful sounds was the music from the old pump organ. Not the same person, but someone was usually there to play the organ. Those persons who played it had learned to play while attending the Episcopal boarding school. We sang Christian hymns that had been translated into Dakota. The older people had committed most of them to memory. We sang loudly, slowly, and in good harmony. Not only did we sing hymns, we also chanted psalms in Dakota. It was a joyful experience even for those who stood outside and listened.

The priest was Father Rouillard. He was a very distinguished-looking man with distinctive American Indian facial features. In addition to his regular clerical garb, he wore a beautiful beaded stole made of white chamois skin, which was draped around his neck and hung gracefully down the front. The cross designs on the stole were made of beads of various colors, which matched the beaded chain that held the cross suspended around his neck. He was one of those priests whom the people loved dearly. One reason was simply the kind person that he was. Another was because he made the announcements, read the scripture and prayers, and delivered the sermon all in Dakota, making the whole worship experience eloquent and meaningful.

After the last hymn and the benediction, people filed out of the church building and lingered outside while the women made their way to the church house where the food was. In a few moments one of the older men came out of the church house and announced that people were to park their cars in a circle to the east of the church. When this was done, everyone began unpacking the plates, cups, bowls, and silverware they had brought. Blankets and quilts of all colors and sizes were spread on the ground inside the perimeter of the circle. Families and extended families sat together. When the dinner was in honor of someone, that person and his or her family sat in the middle of the circle and were served first, but today there were no particular honorees.

The servers were usually the younger women and teenage girls. This was not easy for the teenagers because most of them were very shy. But they did their best. There was always more food than we could eat. Some of the foods were combined in big dishpans to make it easier and quicker to serve. All the cakes were cut and put into one pan. This also gave everyone a choice as to what kind of cake they wanted. The pies were cut and served in the same manner. The breads were mixed as was the fried chicken. Several large kettles of chicken soup were taken around and served at the same time. Then the huge pots of Kool-aid, tea, and coffee were poured. It was amazing how quickly everyone was served and ready to eat.

Sometime in the middle of the serving, the priest would have everyone stand and sing the doxology in Dakota. I looked forward to that. The voices blended so well, with each note bouncing off the metal doors of the cars. When we finished, he prayed a prayer of thanksgiving. Then the servers continued to pass the food around. The men and boys sometimes did things in the background but never served the food.

It was a beautiful sight, people sitting on the ground, on the car fenders and running boards, people of all ages sitting together. The youth and little ones always tried to sit with the grandmas in the crowd. There was something sacred and tender about what we were experiencing, almost like Holy Communion: people breaking bread, sharing food and their lives with each other. It was an event that etched itself deeply in everyone's memory.

Before the meal ended, someone would stand near the center of the circle to thank everyone for coming and bringing food. Then that person would reminisce about other celebrations and people who were "no longer with us." The speaker would name some of them. Usually they were well-known members of the church and community. Some people continued to eat slowly and quietly, while others stopped eating to listen. Everyone, however, either looked down toward the ground or closed their eyes while listening, which was a sign of respect for the speaker, what he was saying, and for the person he was talking about.

He began by saying, "Mitakuyapi" ("You're all my relatives"). And all the older men or leaders confirmed it by saying, "Hau." When he was finished, he would end his message by saying, "Hecetu" ("So it is"). And the other men once more responded with "Hau." Usually it turned out to be a thought-provoking and affirming speech.

In the Sioux culture we have the word "wateca." It refers to food that is left over after a meal. After a dinner such as this one, everyone is welcome to take home some of the leftovers, at least in moderation. That is because when a person brings food for such an occasion it becomes community property. In addition, when food that someone has brought is all gone by the end of the feast or is taken home as "wateca," it is considered a compliment.

When everyone was through eating that day, some took their own cake pans or plates and went into the church house, where the remaining food was. They took whatever they wanted for a meal later that day. This behavior was acceptable and expected. Nobody packed up their pans and food until everyone had taken what they wanted.

One woman in the community was not a very good cook. In fact there were those who referred to her as "a terrible cook." Consequently, when everyone went to get "wateca," no one took any of hers. Grandma, being the sensitive and caring person that she was, noticed that the woman's feelings were hurt by this. Grandma very diplomatically went to her and asked, "Did you bring those raisin pies over there?" "Yes, I did," she answered. "Is it all right," Grandma went on, "if I take some home?" Her face brightening, she said, "Why of course!" (This was all said in Dakota.) She immediately helped Grandma bundle them up.

Occasionally someone would offer us a ride home after the church service or a dinner such as this one, but today no one did. Grandma never seemed to mind walking, and of course David and I didn't mind.

The afternoon was lovely. It was now about two o'clock. The sun was still high but beginning to descend. There was only a slight breeze and had been ever since we went to help Mrs. Ree. As we walked together, we talked about what we had experi-

119

enced so far that day. Making our way down the long hill toward our house, we looked for wild turnips (which weren't really turnips at all, but a prairie plant that American Indians used for food). When we found one, we took the time to look for its mate, which was always nearby. We didn't dig them up because it was next to impossible to do so without a turnip digger, the root was buried so deep.

When we got to the bottom of the hill, Grandma wanted to stop and rest for a while. As we sat in the shade under the big lone cottonwood tree David said he was hungry. He wanted to know what Grandma was bringing home. Without saying a word Grandma untied her bundle of dishes, pans, and dish towels. There was some fried chicken, a few pieces of different kinds of cake, and four raisin pies, already cut. David took the first piece of pie and tasted it. "Not bad," he said. We began to eat pie. When we finished, David and I had eaten two raisin pies.

"It's time to go," Grandma said. "Your Grandpa will be looking for us." And he was. After being home alone all day, he was always glad to see us and made us feel welcome.

We had had a good day. Alex had too. He had left the house before us but didn't get back until after we had been home for a while. He went through the whole day without getting into any trouble, as far as we knew.

I had the feeling of having been to church. It was a clean feeling. The whole day had been spiritually uplifting. The unexpected had happened at the most unexpected time—that morning the touch on my shoulder, the sliding of a prayer book in front of me. It was events like this that began to set my life on a certain course.

13

Living with my grandparents in that little house on Choteau Creek was not all fun and feasting. There was work to be done in order to survive. We had to be creative and constructive and make the best of what we had. With so little, we had to use wisely what we had and that which was given to us.

Grandma had only one blood relative of her generation who was still living. Her name was Alice Gray. Grandma always said that they were cousins. She never described Alice as a first, second, or third cousin, because in the Sioux culture that is inappropriate. The proper term in these cases is "cousin," that's all.

In addition, in Sioux culture there are claimed relatives, what sociologists call fictive kin. They are relatives in a cultural and social sense, but not biologically or legally. It is a kinship that is beyond even the extended family. If, for example, an old woman comes up to me and greets me and tells me she is my grandmother, that is accepted without question. She accepts an obligation to be my grandmother. It is a claimed relationship.

This was not the way it was between Grandma and Alice Gray. According to Grandma, Alice was a blood relative. Because they were "the last ones left," they kept in touch with each other. When Grandma was younger and her eyesight was better, she used to write to Alice once a month or so. Now that it was hard for her to see well enough to write, they corresponded only about once a year.

It was fascinating to watch Grandma write. She had her own tablet, the kind she gave to me at Christmas. It was a small tablet without lines, but the first page had heavy, dark lines and she put it under the page on which she was writing. As her eyesight deteriorated she was able to follow those lines less and less well. Before ballpoint pens were available, she used an indelible pencil. It was her pencil and no one else used it. Now and then she would lick the tip of the pen. It must have worked better that way. By the time she finished her letter there was a purple spot on her tongue.

Grandma had very elaborate handwriting, unlike any I have ever seen before or since. The top part of her capital "J" looked like a fancy triangle, for example. Her upper-case "D" had an intricate tail that went high above the letter. The small "s" reminded me of a small, fancy triangle. The last letter of every sentence had a decorative tail. Her periods at the end of each sentence were little circles. When I watched her write a letter, even from across the room, I could tell when she came to the end of a sentence.

If I listened closely, which I never did for any length of time, I knew what she was writing, because she whispered every word as she wrote it. She even ended the last word in each sentence abruptly while adding the fancy tail.

Alice and John Gray lived near Greenwood, a small village on the Missouri River about thirty-five miles away. Because of the long distance, Grandma and Alice saw each other about once a year. Either Grandma would make arrangements to go there, or they would come to our house to visit for a day. I saw Alice only twice in my lifetime. She was of medium height and a bit on the heavy side. Her beautiful white hair blended well with her tan-brown skin and looked so nice with her rimless glasses. In spite of the difference in their build and weight, she and Grandma shared a remarkable resemblance in their facial features and gestures. They were blood relatives, for sure.

Whenever they visited each other it was usually on a day when David and I were in school. I didn't even know when they were coming to our house, or when Grandma was going to visit them, until it was over. One day when Grandma returned from visiting Alice and John Gray, she brought an old hen and four chicks which they had given to her. Along with the chickens they gave her a small bag of feed and a small bag of shelled corn.

The first night we kept the the chickens in a big cardboard box on the porch. We went to the straw stack in the field behind the house to get straw for their nest. The next day we cleaned out an old junk box, covered the front with some old pieces of boards, and made a small door. We put more fresh straw in this old box as a nesting place for the hen and her four little ones. It became their permanent home until they outgrew it.

Grandma knew how to care for chickens. This soon became apparent as they began to grow and multiply. In a short time we had to use the dog house for a chicken coop.

One day when I returned home from school, I discovered to my surprise that Dan and Maggie Jandreau had given Grandpa and Grandma an old shed, which they moved down to the house with a team of horses and a wagon. How they moved it and un-loaded it, I never knew. We made it into a chicken coop by build-ing some roosts and nests in it. It had enough room for thirty to forty chickens. I discovered very soon that chickens are smart. It didn't take long to teach them where to go when it began to get dark. After they were herded into the coop about three nights in a row, they began to go in by themselves.

It wasn't long before there were more chickens than there was room in the chicken coop. We went back to using the old junk box for some of them. Sometime later we built another box to hold a few more chickens. Out of that first little flock Grandma raised over six hundred chickens. We had boiled eggs, fried eggs, scrambled eggs, and plenty of them. We also had fried chicken, baked chicken, and chicken soup whenever we wanted it, as long as Grandma hadn't named the chicken. Any chicken that had a name was exempt from being eaten.

It was my job to clean the chicken coop, sometimes to feed them and gather the eggs, and to make sure the doors were closed up tight and wired shut every evening. Grandma use to say, "Be sure the doors are shut tight so nobody can get in." When she said that, I use to think, "Grandma, nobody is going to walk way down here during the night to get into our chicken coop." And then I remembered her prayers, and how she prayed for the care and safety of all the animals and the birds. I discovered that Grandma was referring to the fox, the raccoon, the mink, and the skunk. To Grandma, all these animals were "somebody."

Very early one morning the chickens began to fuss. Before anybody else realized it, Grandma got out of bed and went out to the chicken coop. She knew that "somebody" was in there. She waited just outside the door until it came out. It was a mink, and it was not aware of Grandma's presence. When it came out, she grabbed it around the neck and stepped on the rest of its body at the same time. That was a brave thing to do, because minks are notoriously vicious when cornered. She held her hands tight around its neck until it was motionless and limp. When she dropped it, one of the dogs grabbed it and made sure it didn't move any more, ever. When it was all over, she saw that the mink had bitten her on her wrist. Its teeth had punctured her flesh but there was only slight bleeding. Grandma didn't think it was necessary to go to the doctor. She was right, but she was lucky. She had protected her chickens, destroyed their predator, and didn't get sick from the injury. Above all, she had demonstrated her courage. I admired her for it.

Other people admired and respected her, too. Nearly all the young Indians called her "Grandma Bessie." The middle-aged Indians referred to her as "Aunt Bessie." All the white people in the community who knew her addressed her as "Mrs. Bourissau."

People came from all over and asked, "Aunt Bessie, could we buy some eggs?" And Grandma would respond, "No, you can have them. How many do you need?" Still others came to our place and asked, "Mrs. Bourissau, could we buy a couple chickens?" Again she would answer, "No, you can have them."

Grandma never sold an egg or a chicken. She always gave them away. I thought to myself, "Grandma, why don't you take them up on their offer to pay for the eggs and chickens? You could use that money to buy something for yourself, or Grandpa, or even for me." But she always gave them away, regardless who was asking. Then one day I understood why she did it. To one farm couple who came to buy a few dozen eggs, she said, "No," with a little chuckle, "you can just have them. God gave to me so I could give to you." That's what Grandma believed, and she lived according to her beliefs.

Other people came to the house just to visit Grandma and Grandpa. Before they left, Grandma and Grandpa always gave them something to take home with them. In the summertime, if they didn't give away eggs, they gave away fresh vegetables from their garden.

One of the things I enjoyed about the spring of the year was the chance to help Grandpa rake the garden clean and burn all that was left from fall. There were the dried-up vines from the cucumbers and squash. The old cornstalks were still standing, for the most part. The tops of the potato and tomato plants still lay where they were left. All of this in addition to the grass that was left to grow during the late summer and fall was raked into a big pile near the middle of the garden and burned. The crackling of the fire reminded me that there was still life in those old vines and stalks and that with each crackle the life was bursting loose into the universe. And the wonderful aroma of the smoke made me believe that it was purifying the air all around us so that new life could begin again.

Then came the long and tedious task of preparing the soil for planting. Grandpa did most of it. He usually worked on it while David and I were in school. Using what he called a potato digger, he carefully turned the soil. His potato digger was a sort of cross between a spade and a pitchfork. It had a relatively short shaft with a handle on the end of it. The fork part had four tines that were flat on the front and rounded on the back.

Grandpa worked slowly and steadily, turning each forkful and hitting it once or twice to break it into smaller chunks. If I was around, I could hear him breathing nearly all the way across the garden. There was that rhythm again, just as when he shoveled snow. He pressed the fork down into the ground with his right foot, at a certain angle that always looked the same each time. Push it down, turn the dirt, push it down, turn the dirt, over and over, doing almost perfect squares each time. Even though they planted a big garden, it took Grandpa only a few days to work the soil.

In the middle of the morning, while Grandpa was working in the garden, he would call to David or me, "Bring me a dipper of water." One of us would take the big green dipper, about half full of water, out to him. Every time before he took a drink, he would pour some of the water out onto the ground, then he would drink the rest. That was Grandpa's way of thanking God and giving some of it back to Mother Earth.

Grandma and Grandpa planted the garden and I helped them keep it clean. In the middle of the summer, when there was no rain, we carried water from the creek to give the plants a drink. I loved watching them grow.

People came from near and far and Grandpa and Grandma gave them squash, cucumbers, tomatoes, potatoes, onions, and radishes. Again, when they could have sold their produce they chose to give it away.

Early in the morning after they had been to town, before I was out of bed, I could hear Grandpa and Grandma, either in the old kitchen or out on the porch, visiting. At that hour I was always sure their hands weren't idle. They had been out in the garden already and back. As they visited they shelled peas, stemmed and broke green beans, and cleaned carrots and turnips. They were getting ready to make a big kettle of vegetable soup, using the beef ribs they had purchased the day before.

When they cooked something special, and this soup was always special, Grandma used to wish someone would come to visit us so we could share it with company. Sometimes someone did come before the soup was ready, and other times we ate it by ourselves.

Grandpa was not always eager to share Grandma's cooking with company, at least not like she was. And then there were times when the meat was not as tender as Grandma thought it should be. At those times she would say rather apologetically, "The meat is kind of tough." Grandpa always responded by saying, "Damn sight tougher when you don't have it."

In spite of his reluctance to share Grandma's cooking with others, when company was present he would go into great detail as to how the meal came to be. It seemed to be his way of saying,

127

"While we had a part in it, we didn't do it alone," and he was always thankful.

They put so much of themselves into everything they did that giving must have been a form of sharing something very personal with others. They shared because they were thankful, and they gave because God gave to them. They gave and gave because that's just the way Grandpa and Grandma were.

14

One could say the summer of 1951 was a summer of signs and wonders. It was while living in that old house on Choteau Creek that I learned to think in terms of our togetherness and our place in the universe. Grandma thought of the birds and other animals as "somebody" with purpose and value, so much so that she devoted a great deal of her prayer life to them. During severe thunderstorms it was not unusual to find her kneeling beside her bed praying for the safety of the birds and wild animals.

The message from the owl had meaning for her. When the old owl landed on the housetop it brought a message that was serious enough to cause worry and become a prayerful concern for Grandma. Not unlike us, the owl was a part of the universe and had a purpose. One of its purposes was to warn people.

For Grandma and Grandpa those persons whom we refer to as "the dead" are more alive than we know. They are alive in the sense that they continue to love us as persons and care about what happens to us here on earth. The relationship with those whom we call "dead" continues to grow, even to the degree that from time to time they come to visit us.

My maternal grandparents were the only grandparents I ever knew. My paternal grandfather was the first full-blooded Yankton Sioux to graduate from the University of South Dakota. He graduated from law school in 1909 and became an attorney. In October 1933, seven years before I was born, he was killed in an automobile accident. My paternal grandmother died when I was about two years old. She was a very traditional American Indian who had long braids, always wore moccasins, and could not speak English. I recall seeing her just once. She came to my crib, looked at me, then turned around and walked away. I do not remember what she looked like, but I do remember her two long braids and the shawl that she was wearing. Grandma talked about her often. She always told me that my paternal grandmother was a very pretty woman.

One night I was awakened by the sound of footsteps in the kitchen. They were soft and slow. The sound was one that I imagined to be made by someone wearing soft leather moccasins. The sound came closer and closer. I lay in my bed staring at the ceiling and wondering what was causing the noise. After a few moments I worked up enough courage to look around. I saw the image of a woman standing beside my bed, looking at me. She just looked for a few seconds. Then she turned around and looked at Grandma's sewing machine for a few moments. When she did that, I could see her braids and what appeared to be a shawl draped over her shoulders. She turned to her right and looked at the dresser beside my bed. She did not appear to be looking for something specific. She was just looking. Finally she turned in my direction again, stood there for a while, then began walking out of the room into the kitchen. When she faced my direction the last time, I couldn't see her hands because they were inside her shawl. Neither could I make out any distinct facial features.

When she was out of sight I could still hear her footsteps, like soft, smooth leather sliding on the floor. The sound continued until it reached the door between the winter kitchen and the old kitchen. Then it stopped. Lying there in the dark, I wasn't afraid, but it was mysterious. Who was that woman, and what was the meaning of her visit? I continued to lie there, wondering, until I went back to sleep.

The next morning I said nothing to anyone about my mysterious visitor. I wondered if Grandma had heard the footsteps and seen the woman. I knew Grandpa hadn't, because I could hear him snore while it was all happening. But Grandma, I didn't know if she had been awake or not. I went through the whole day thinking about this experience. Several times I almost said something to both Grandma and Grandpa, but the timing didn't seem right, so I waited.

That night while Grandpa was sleeping and Grandma and I were sitting in the old kitchen, she settled down in her usual posture of thought and storytelling. Again she put her left arm across her lap, placed her right elbow in her left hand, and partially covered her closed eyes and her forehead with her right hand. There were a few minutes of complete silence. Before she could say anything, I said, "Grandma, there was an old woman who came to my bed last night." I described how she had looked at me, then at the sewing machine and the dresser. I described the sound, like moccasins on the floor.

Grandma didn't appear shocked or surprised. Without moving a muscle or opening her eyes, she said, "That must have been your Grandma Rock Boy coming to visit you." That was all she said. I waited for her to attach some meaning to her visit, but she didn't. She just sat there in her thoughtful position.

"Grandma," I asked, "why would Grandma Rock Boy come to see me?" "They do that, you know," she responded, "because they are concerned and care about you."

Grandma didn't say much more the rest of the night. Perhaps she was giving it some thought. Nothing happened as a result of the visit, at least nothing that we could connect to it. I never saw Grandma Rock Boy again.

What amazed me was Grandma's calmness. It was like another visitor who just showed up. It confirmed her belief that the dead never really die. The relationship with them continues to grow and becomes deeper and deeper.

Several evenings later, Grandma sat in her usual position in the old kitchen. The day had been long and hot. But now, in the coolness of the evening, she and I sat and talked about important and mundane things, serious and funny matters. Then the expression appeared that always showed on her face as she slipped into another time in thought and feeling. It was her son this time of whom she was thinking. He was Grandma and Grandpa's firstborn child. He had died forty years before, when he was only one year old. Grandpa never talked about him. Grandma, however, shared lots of fond memories of him. His first language, like Grandma's, was Dakota Sioux. With a twinkle in her eyes and a smile on her face she told about how he used to mispronounce certain words as he was learning to talk.

This evening she talked about how he walked and how assertive he was. In the evening twilight I could see how misty-eyed she had become. "If my son didn't die when he was a baby," she said, "if he had lived to be an adult and was still alive, I believe he would have gone into the army and made it a career." There was a pause. Then she said, "But he didn't live very long." She reached for her handkerchief and began to wipe the moistness from her eyes.

How Grandma had come to this conclusion I never knew. And if it had anything to do with the events that were to follow, that too is uncertain. Not much more was said as the shadows lengthened and disappeared and our busy world was hushed.

Several days later, in the middle of the afternoon, Grandpa decided to sit for a while on the east side of the house where it was cooler. Grandma, who had remained inside, was sitting on the edge of her bed in her silent and thoughtful manner, while I was in the other room reading an old sports magazine that we had gotten from someone. Suddenly I heard Grandma talking to someone. "Well, here's my son!" she said. "You have come to visit me!" There was a brief moment of silence. Then she cried out in excitement and joy, "My son, my son!" and began to cry. She didn't wail and chant like she did at the cemetery. No, these were sobs that came from the very core of her being, letting out feelings of pain and grief that had been buried there for years.

Rushing to her side and gently putting my hand on her back, I asked, "Grandma, what happened?" Although the tears still streamed down her cheeks, she calmed down enough to reply in a soft and shaky voice, "My son came to visit me. I saw him. He was standing right here," pointing in front of her. "He had on an army uniform," she went on, "with lots of ribbons. I could see them going up his left shoulder." Burying her eyes in her handkerchief, she sobbed, "I reached out to touch him, but he was gone." And she cried some more.

There was the sound of the screen door opening and closing and the heavy, uneven thumps of Grandpa's footsteps and his cane. Coming into the room, he asked, "What is wrong, my dear?" He stood in front of Grandma, his eyes open wide and his face turning pale as she described what had happened. He sat down in his rocking chair but continued to gaze at her. Then he sniffed. His eyes filled with tears and one big drop ran down his cheek. He didn't even try to hide it. He sniffed again. With the back of his hand he wiped the tear that hung on the edge of his jaw. There was a presence in the room that I hadn't sensed the night Grandma Rock Boy came to visit me. It was heavy and intense. It would have been difficult to miss. There had to be some message in this sign. But what?

For the remainder of that day and for the next few days a shadow hung over the house, and the darkness was reflected in Grandpa and Grandma's mood and actions. A sense of foreboding prevailed in all of us. Grandpa turned off the radio before the baseball game was over. It evidently was hard for him to concentrate. Grandma didn't laugh and play with the dogs and cats. She was impatient with the chickens at feeding time. It was very clear that something heavy was in their hearts.

On the third day after Grandma's vision, she decided to walk up to the church and clean the sanctuary. David and I decided to tag along. In the middle of the morning Grandma gathered some cleaning rags, a towel or two, a small jar of soap, and an old basin. She put them all in a flour sack that had been emptied and washed, and we set off for the church. It was a happy and carefree day for two of the dogs, Tizer and Alex, because Grandma didn't insist that they stay at home. Although Ohitika was the same age as Alex, and in fact they were brothers, he never seemed to have as much strength and energy as Alex did. Or maybe he was just more serious and sensible. He didn't always try to follow us when we went somewhere. This was one of those days when he wanted to stay at home.

It was a hot, humid morning. We made our way down the road, across the dam, and up the hill with the dogs several yards ahead of us. We could hear the rustling of the corn leaves blowing in the wind. At times we could hear the wind but not feel it. We paused occasionally and waited for the wind, but it passed by without touching our faces. A couple of times we stopped to looked for some gum on the big sunflowers. We didn't find very much, at least not enough to chew; just a taste. The dogs scared up a pheasant hen from her nest and, later, a flock of quail along the way. They seemed to think they had done a day's work with

134

that. When we reached the top of the hill, still half a mile from the church, we could begin to feel a fresh breeze.

Arriving at the church, we used the old hand pump to draw water for Grandma to clean with and some for us to drink after the long, hot walk. First Grandma swept the floor, next she washed the woodwork and the stained-glass windows, and then she carefully dusted all the furniture. The last things she worked on were the heavy candleholders and the cross. She polished them until they shone like mirrors. Before packing up her cleaning equipment, she called David and me in to inspect the place and tell her which places she had missed.

After everything was done and we were ready to begin the long walk home, Grandma walked to the altar rail and knelt down in her same prayerful position as she did every Sunday morning, her hands covering both eyes and her forehead. She remained there for a long while. I sat down in one of the pews toward the back of the church, watching and waiting. The silence was almost complete. The only sounds were the wind and the building cracking from time to time. In my mind I could almost hear Grandma's silent prayer. With the heavy cloud that had been hanging over her and Grandpa ever since she saw their son, there was no doubt that she was deeply involved with her prayer concerns. As she knelt there, motionless, her back to me, it was quite apparent that she was in another world. How long she remained that way, no one knows. There was no clock in the church building and none of us had watches. Time was not a very influencing factor in our lives, anyway. There were other things that helped to govern our lives, things like the length of daylight, the position of the sun, the amount of dew on the grass, and the temperature.

When Grandma finished her prayer, she stood up, turned in my direction, and began to wipe away the tiny beads of perspiration from her forehead and around her eyes. Walking to where I was sitting in the back of the church, she stopped and placed a hand on my shoulder and said, "Come, let's go home now." It was as though it took courage for her to go home.

The way home consisted mostly of trails. The roads themselves were little more than two tracks, one for each tire, with weeds between them. Grandma walked on one side and David on the other, beside her, while I walked behind David. The two dogs went ahead of us, one on each side. They would trot a ways ahead, then wait for us to catch up to them.

Grandma was in a hurry to get home. The heaviness that hung over her mind and in her soul was evidenced by the way she walked. She continued at a steady, fast pace, as she had the morning David and Dorothy left, and when Clement Good Teacher was sick. With each step her wide, thick heel resounded against the hard, dry dirt of the road.

From the top of the hill it seemed like we could see forever. The fields and rolling hills stretched to the east for miles and miles. We could see only the green roof of our house with its brick chimney in the center. Grandma stood there with her hands on her hips, gazing into the distance. Her poor eyesight prevented her from seeing much, but she seemed to take pleasure in what she could make of it.

Just as we started down the winding path toward the dam, David and I could see a car driving away from the house. Before I could say anything, he said, "Grandma, there is a black car coming from the house." "Whose is it?" she asked. "I don't know," he responded. "I don't recognize the car." Probably he and I were thinking the same thing—"Maybe somebody brought Mom home"—but it was never spoken.

By this time the dogs were quite a distance ahead of us. The closer we got to the house the farther ahead of us they were. The car went past the dam, over the hill to the north, and out of sight long before we could get near the road to the house. When we

136

reached the dam, we began to examine the tire tracks. They weren't any that we recognized. We hurried on, anxious to know who was at the house and who we had missed.

Arriving home, David set Grandma's cleaning supplies on the table in the old kitchen. By then it was late afternoon. From the east windows and the open door, the shadow of the house was noticeably long. It reached almost to the garden. We all walked into the room where Grandpa was sitting in his rocking chair beside the radio. The radio was turned off. Except for our footsteps the house was quiet. Grandma went in first, then I, and behind me, David followed. Grandma sat on their bed, near the foot, the same place she was sitting when she had the vision of her son.

"Who was here?" she asked. Looking in the direction of David and me, Grandpa said, "Your Aunt Lucy and Roy were here. They just left." He continued, "They brought some bad news." His voice got louder and very firm, as though he was trying to hide his emotions. "Phillip was wounded in Korea and they have sent him to Tokyo. From there they will ship him to San Antonio, Texas."

While he spoke he kept looking at Grandma, and Grandma was staring at the floor. His voice became weak and shaky as he said, "This happened on Tuesday. He was shot in the neck."

There were a few moments of dead silence: no birds singing, no chickens cackling, no dogs barking, no wind blowing—just silence. Then Grandma broke down and began to cry. She sobbed just as she had a few days before. She cried, "Oh, my grandson, my grandson," and her tears poured forth.

Grandpa just sat there like he was stunned. He continued to look at Grandma with his eyes wide open. This time there were no tears in his eyes. He sniffed a few times and the right side of his mouth and his cheek quivered, but that was all. He managed to control his emotions. Perhaps he did so for Grandma's sake, or for all of us. When he felt he had to be strong, he was strong. This must have been one of those times.

When Grandma stopped crying, she said, "I knew something bad was going to happen." That was all she said. She just sat there staring at the floor.

I couldn't believe what was happening. I imagined Phillip lying out on some battlefield in Korea. This had happened several days ago. Maybe by now he was dead. He was only eighteen years old. He had enlisted in the army when he was only seventeen. I was too shocked to cry or say anything. We all were. We just sat there thinking our own thoughts and feeling our own pain. Maybe no one said anything because there was nothing to say. We sat there, all of us.

The shadow of the house lengthened and began to merge with its surroundings in the dusk. It would soon be time to light the lamp. Finally Grandma got up and began to clean the lamp chimney, trying to make things brighter in the dimness of our lives. She polished the glass chimney until it was time to light the lamp. Her effort was not in vain, for the chimney was crystal clear and the lamplight shone brighter because of it.

There in the coolness of the night as the stars began peeping out from the deep purple sky, a presence was felt that enabled us to believe that those persons whom we think of as dead come to visit us in the middle of the day or night. Sometimes they come because they care and are concerned. Other times they come to bring a message and provide a sign.

15

Laughter and love were elements that permeated our day-to-day experience. A sense of humor is an important characteristic of American Indian cultures. We believe there is a fine line between laughter and tears. They are both enabling means of survival. Having lived at a high economic level during the early years of their marriage, Grandpa and Grandma had lost their farm during the Great Depression and had since lived on bare necessities. While continuously trying the make the adjustment, they used laughter as a way of cultivating faith and hope.

Grandma was among the most gentle and compassionate people who ever lived. Behind her seriousness, however, there was a keen sense of humor. She liked to laugh and joke. She would tease the cats, the dogs, and me. She never made fun of a person, although she made jokes about what it meant to be an Indian, which is typical of American Indian humor.

Grandma was loved by everyone, even the animals. There must have been moments when she wished she wasn't loved, especially by the chickens. She couldn't go outside without all the animals coming to her. When we didn't know where she was, we used to say, "Just look for the dogs and cats and a flock of chickens; Grandma will be somewhere near."

Of course, she was the one who fed and cared for the animals. All a person had to do was slam the front door and all the animals would come running. When they saw it wasn't Grandma, they went back, in apparent disgust, to what they had been doing.

Grandma took great care in cooking for the dogs and cats. A few times, unknown to her, David and I tasted what she was preparing for them. We thought it didn't taste too bad. If Grandma had only known what we were up to, she would have thought it was funny and probably would have offered the food to us. When she dished out their food and set it in front of them, they would eat with such gusto that they made it look even better. Occasionally two of the dogs would fight over each other's food. If Grandma was nearby, she would not hesitate to step in between them. They would stop fighting immediately. Then she would give them a long lecture about fighting. The more she lectured, the more embarrassed and ashamed they appeared to be. If it was the two big dogs fighting, she said things like, "You two are brothers, and brothers shouldn't be fighting like that." Or if it was Tizer and Alex who were fighting—and Alex was usually one of them—Grandma would say to them, "Goodness, you shouldn't be fighting each other. Alex, you should be ashamed of yourself for fighting someone so much smaller than you." They understood every word she spoke.

She sat under the trees during the summer months and laughed and played with the animals. She talked for the animals and thereby had them talking to each other. Again, they seem to understand what they were supposed to be saying and to whom they were supposed to be saying it. Grandma even had the dogs and cats joking with each other. She delighted in the animals, and the sound of laughter at times could be heard at a considerable distance.

Grandma very seldom lost her temper. Even when she was annoyed she could usually manage to control it. And she would never dream of swearing. Not once did she resort to what were known as "bad words." Her vocabulary was large enough, even though English was her second language, that she could express herself in a rational and intelligent manner without using "bad words."

As time went on, two things began to happen in Grandpa's life. He slept more during each day, and he began to lose his temper more, about little things, even toward Grandma.

One day Grandma and I decided to wash some clothes. We hauled and heated the water and did all that had to be done prior to the actual washing. Grandpa slept through most of this activity, noisy as we were. When we were ready to wash the jeans and overalls, Grandma walked to their bed, woke Grandpa, and asked if there was anything in particular that he needed to have washed. He calmly said, "I would like to have washed the overalls that I took off yesterday." So Grandma searched through the laundry bag until she found them. She then showed them to him and asked, "Are these the ones that you want washed?" He rose halfway from his pillow and very impatiently said, "No. I want you to wash the overalls that I took off yesterday!" At that Grandma bristled and leaned forward, then shouted, "These are the ones you took off yesterday, you old son of a gun!"

They were both shocked. He was shocked to hear her talk like that, and she was shocked to think that she would resort to that kind of language. They both stared at each other for a few moments, then burst out laughing. Grandpa put his head on his pillow and went back to sleep.

Before Grandpa's health began to give way, he spent much of his time down by the creek. In the fall of the year he was cutting down dead trees and dragging them up to the house to be used for fuel. During the cold winter months, he could be found chopping ice and carrying it to the house in a big galvanized tub to be melted for our household water supply. It was no easy task. When spring overcame the sharpness of winter, he sometimes walked the banks of the creek watching the water rise and the ice break up into large cakes that floated downstream. And the warmth of the summer, when it was in full bloom, continuously called him to his special places where he fished for enough bullheads and carp for supper.

For many years he used a heavy ash pole as the major part of his fishing equipment. When he was ready, David and I carried his equipment to where he intended to fish. It consisted of the big pole with the line, bobber, hook, and sinker on it, the large pail that he sat on, his can of worms and grasshoppers, and a burlap bag in which he kept the fish he caught. Sometimes we would fish alongside him. When we didn't, he would say, "Come back about noon. I may be ready to come home by then." One or both of us would return and help him bring his catch and equipment home.

One day Grandpa came back from town with a new wagon, large enough for two children to ride in. It was made of wood and had six sideboards that could be removed; three of them were red and the other three had a natural finish. We used it to haul his fishing equipment to the creek and back. In addition, while he was fishing he sat in it. That was the main purpose for which he bought it.

But out of the goodness of his heart and because we were his boys, he let David and me play with it when he wasn't using it. It gave us hours of fun. We would take it to the very top of the hill west of the house and take turns riding down the hill at top speed. One of us would ride while the other would make sure the rider was off to a flying start. In order not to run into the porch, we had to make a sharp right turn and continue down the road or between the ash pile and the plum bushes just south of the house. A few times we barely made the turn, missing the porch by a hair. Of course, we didn't say much about our activity because Grandpa might think we were playing too rough with his wagon. He wasn't supposed to know about it.

We continued this amusement until we noticed that the rubber tires were showing signs of rolling off the wheel rims in the same direction as the sharp right turns we were making. For sure, we would hear from Grandpa about this.

One evening while Grandpa was sitting on the porch, he began to look over the wagon, which David was sitting in, directly in front of him. Grandpa observed, "What happened to the tires on the wagon? They're coming off. That's caused by you boys making those fast, sharp turns with it."

I didn't know what to say, so David spoke up, "No, Grandpa, that's caused by you sitting in it on a slant while you're fishing." Grandpa replied simply, "That's what you think."

I don't think he believed us, but we were not sure. Maybe he wasn't sure either. Nevertheless, that was all that was said, and we weren't banned from playing with the wagon and he continued to sit on a slant while fishing.

When Grandpa decided to go fishing, at breakfast he would say, "One of you boys dig some worms for me and the other one catch some grasshoppers for me." Digging for worms didn't take long, but finding and catching grasshoppers took forever, it seemed. That had to be the worst job. We caught only the big hoppers and put them in one of Grandpa's empty tobacco cans.

To our surprise, one summer, Grandpa bought a new rod and reel for himself. It was a beauty. David and I couldn't wait to get our hands on it, but for a long while the only person who did get his hands on it was Grandpa. Although he never did really learn how to use it, he enjoyed it.

Using a rod and reel was much different from using his ash pole. When he caught a big fish with his old pole, he would stand up and throw the fish up on the bank. When he started using his new reel, he pulled the fish in close to the shore, then picked it up. There were a few times when his catch was too heavy for his thin rod. Then, if one of us boys was there, we would go down to the edge of the water, pick up the fish, and unhook it for him.

One morning, while Grandpa and I were fishing, it was apparent that he had a big one on the end of his line. He struggled just to get it to the shore. Grandpa's eyes were big, his mouth open, and leaning back with his rod bent, he fought to win the battle. Hurrying down the bank, I waited until he had it there in front of me. It was the largest catfish I had ever seen. Reaching down, I pulled it out of the water and held it up to show it to Grandpa. He exclaimed excitedly, "There's enough there for all of us to eat!"

I began to take the hook out of its mouth. Just as I got it out, the fish began to struggle. I hung on as tight as I could, but it was quicker and stronger than I. It slipped out of my hands, splashed back into the water, and swiftly swam away. I knew Grandpa would be disappointed and was afraid he would be upset with me.

Frowning a little, he asked, "Did you get hurt?" "No," I answered timidly. With his hand-rolled cigarette hanging out one side of his mouth, he smiled widely and said, "That was the grandma. Now we'll catch the grandpa." That was all he said. He didn't catch the grandpa that day, but nothing more was ever said.

There were times when Grandpa's sense of humor far exceeded that which anyone had the right to expect. One of those times was one morning following a heavy nighttime rainstorm. Grandpa and I went walking down by the creek to see if the storm had done any damage. One of the first things we noticed was that a small tree had fallen into the water where the bank had washed away from under it. Grandpa decided to salvage the trunk for firewood, so after lunch he grabbed his ax and headed back to the creek.

Thinking that it was going to take him quite a while to finish the job, I took one of the old tires I used to roll around as an imaginary car. When we got back to where the tree was lying in the water, Grandpa slid down the bank and stood on a little ledge bordering the water and began to chop away at the tree.

While he was busy at his task, I was busy rolling my tire around, up and down the creek bank. I was able to get the tire rolling so fast that at times I could hardly keep up with it. A few times the tire did roll faster than I could run, but before long it would slow down and I would catch up with it.

One of those times, however, the tire got to traveling faster and faster, right out of control. To my dismay, it rolled straight toward where Grandpa was chopping on the tree. I ran as fast as I could, and almost caught it once, but my legs wouldn't continue to carry me fast enough. It was too late, and there wasn't anything I could do about it. Grandpa was going to get it now and I would surely get it later on.

In that split second, Grandpa happened to be leaning over. The tire rolled off the bank, bounced off Grandpa's back, high into the air, and landed in the water. I wanted to race back to the house and hide behind Grandma but decided I better stay and face the music. Grandpa paused for a moment, trying to figure out what had happened. Then, straightening up and turning in my direction, he smiled and said, "You know, you're one hell of a driver!" And he laughed.

When he finished getting the tree out of the stream, we went back to the house, got his big fishing pole, and Grandpa fished my tire out of the creek. I might have been a "hell of a driver," but he was a wonderful grandpa.

As the years went by, the length of time that he fished grew shorter and shorter and his walks along the banks of the creek became fewer and fewer. His failing health became more evident and his sense of humor began to diminish. The affection and kindness, however, were still there. This was apparent with each cup of coffee that he managed to bring to his and Grandma's bed, but the laughter was gone.

And Grandma—as the light in her eyes grew dimmer and she became more frail in body and mind, she also withdrew into a quietness that was not like herself, at least not the Grandma that I knew and loved. She didn't talk to or play with the animals like she once did. Her laughter became a precious commodity, experienced only once in a while.

It seemed like their laughter was nearly gone and their sense of humor was fading away. It had been there long enough, though, for me to learn it and appreciate it. Their eternal and enduring gift to me was to recognize laughter and a sense of humor as a means of survival. For sure, it worked for them.

16

So much had happened since I first came to live with Grandpa and Grandma. Noticeable and sometimes alarming changes were beginning to take place in those two people whom I loved so much. There were times when Grandpa seemed to get things all mixed up. When this happened it was difficult to help him, because in those moments of confusion he seemed to have a sense of what was happening and it caused him to be afraid. The more I saw him hanging on to the way things used to be, the more I found myself hanging on to that strong and firm Grandpa that I once knew. One thing was becoming clearer: there was going to be a long, rough road ahead for both of us.

For Grandma things were different. She was never afraid of the present or the future; she was her same steady, faithful person—faithful to herself and faithful to others whom she loved. Perhaps this was, at least in part, because she had a strong self-identity; she always seemed to know who she was. And maybe it was because she kept in touch with her beginnings, often taking the time to review and relive her past in mind and spirit.

She would sit, in the evenings, leafing through the pages of her life. Suddenly she would stop, almost as if she had come across something nearly forgotten. She would give a little grunt of surprise, then she would nod her head slightly and cross her feet. She was pondering another of her early experiences and it was apparent that she was about to say something that was worth my undivided attention.

"When I was just a young girl," she began one evening, "I had a nosebleed. It started in the middle of the afternoon, about the same time that your Grandpa's started. It bled most of the afternoon, but by evening it stopped. Before noon the next day, however, it began to bleed again. My father went to the spring and got some cold water. He dipped some rags in the cold water and put them on my forehead and on the back of my neck, thinking that would make it stop bleeding. But it didn't work. My nose kept bleeding throughout most of the afternoon."

She shifted her body in her chair and crossed her feet in the other direction as she rubbed her forehead with the tips of her fingers by slightly nodding her head. In her usual relaxed manner, her eyes closed, she continued: "It was about four o'clock in the afternoon and the sun was beginning to go behind the hill to the west of the house. My parents and I were sitting outside, under the trees. I was holding a rag over my nose and occasionally would hold my head back, hoping to stop the bleeding. Looking to the south, my father said, 'Wana wicaśa wau.' ('A man is coming now'). Someone was coming from the direction of the river. My mother said, 'Wana omani' ('Now someone is wandering around').

We waited for the person to come closer. We could see that he had long braids and was using a long stick for a cane. Slowly he kept walking toward the house. Most of the time he walked with his head bowed down toward the ground. Occasionally he would stop, lift his head, and look around. Now we could see that he was wearing moccasins and was carrying a little leather bag that

148

was strung around his neck with a long leather string. It was apparent that my father and mother didn't recognize him as someone who visited them regularly. Then my father recognized who the visitor was. 'He wicaśa wakan heca,' he said ('He is a medicine man'). Right away my father stood up and went to greet him. After they greeted each other the medicine man said, 'I heard there is someone here who is sick. I came to pray for her.'"

Again Grandma shifted her body and moved her hand away from her forehead. Without opening her eyes, she reached out her hand and said, "He came to where I was sitting and shook my hand. He asked me to remove the cloth I was holding over my nose so he could see. When he saw all the blood, he said, 'Han, śica' ('Yes, too bad')."

Grandma then crossed her arms in front of her as she continued, "First he asked my mother for a blanket he could use. While she was getting the blanket, the medicine man slowly walked around the yard picking up some small branches and twigs that had fallen from the trees. He used these branches to start a fire. As the fire was burning he sat near it with his legs crossed, singing his songs and praying. After the fire burned down and all there was left were some coals, he called me over to the fire. He made me sit down beside the fire, across from him. He sang another song and prayed again. Then he opened the leather bag, and reaching inside, he took out some green herbs and sprinkled them on the coals."

Now Grandma gazed into space without uttering a word. Motioning with both hands, she said, "He took the blanket and threw it over my head and onto my shoulders. He told me to lean forward, over the coals of fire. By that time the herbs began to smoke. When I leaned forward he dropped the other end of the blanket around the edges of the coals. The smoke slowly began to fill the space underneath the blanket. The medicine man told me to take several deep breaths. I did and . . . ," Grandma was now leaning forward with her index finger bent and pointing from her nose toward the floor. She moved her finger in a downward motion as though it were blood dripping from her nose. I sat there counting: one . . . two . . . three . . . four. She looked at me, smiling, and said, "It stopped bleeding."

Stories about the past, sometimes the not-too-distant past, were an important part of her life. They were vivid portrayals of people whose lives had touched her life, or they described a mystical power that filled ordinary, yet not so ordinary, experiences. Some of her stories happened within my lifetime, yet she told and retold them, perhaps to keep them as fresh and alive as at the very moment when they happened.

Like the tragic story about the young boy who drowned in the Missouri River in the fall of 1955. Two teenage boys had been fishing that afternoon. They had just returned to shore, and as they were tying the boat to a small dock it somehow got away from them. One of them dived into the water to bring it back to shore. He came up once, then a second time, and that was the last his friend saw of him. The friend immediately ran for help. People from Greenwood and the surrounding area came to help with what would be a long and painful search for the young boy's body. His parents and brothers and sisters, filled with the fear of the inevitable, walked the banks of the river day and night as the search went on.

After several days of continuous dragging of the river and searching along the shores, whisperings began. People were telling stories about a medicine man who had helped with the search for a little girl who had drowned in the same river, upstream, several months earlier. He had found the little girl's body when no one else could. Stories about the medicine man began to spread.

When the search for the boy began to appear hopeless to the workers, someone began talking about the medicine man openly. A BIA (Bureau of Indian Affairs) policeman who had been present almost constantly began to inquire about this medicine man as he talked with people who stood on the riverbank, watching, waiting, and hoping.

Finally, one of the older men in the group began to speak. "I know this medicine man," he said. "His name is Willie Hanska" (which means Tall Willie). "He is a good man, and would be willing to come here to help us and this grieving family. Of course," he went on, "you know, the family is a strong Catholic family. Before we do anything of this nature, someone should talk with them and get their permission first. That," he said, "would be the respectful thing to do."

There were a few moments of almost complete silence, just the sound of waves slapping against the river bank and the calling of an owl in the distance, up the hill. Then the policeman spoke up, "I would be willing to talk with the family, in private, if it's all right with everyone else." Someone in the background answered, "Han, waśte" ("Yes, that's good"). "It is late, now," the policeman said, "but the first thing in the morning I will visit with the family about this. If they agree to it, I will make the trip to the medicine man's house and talk with him." No one else spoke a word and the people began to move around, which was an indication that the matter had been settled.

Early the next morning the policeman made his way back down to the little village beside the river and straight to the family's house. After a few moments of conversation the family agreed to the idea of enlisting the aid of the medicine man. The policeman immediately began his journey to the medicine man's house, about two hundred miles up the river.

The word spread quickly throughout the village and the surrounding area. Mixed with the sadness of loss, a sense of awe and expectation began to stir in the air. More cars filled with people could be seen coming down the long hill that led to the east end of the village. Some of them followed the rustic road that led to the river bank where people watched the boats going back and forth, up and down the river, dragging the bottom, while others waited their turn to help with the search. Still others drove to the old parish house a few yards west of the little white frame Episcopal church to unload the food they had prepared for the family and workers and, when he arrived, the medicine man.

Some of the women arranged and rearranged the food and dishes in preparation for feeding the workers, while others sat on benches against the walls of the building, visiting. Outside, the children played while the older men stood in groups, talking about ordinary things of life. All of them, however, were waiting in expectation of something awesome, something they believed in but seldom saw happen any more.

Meanwhile, the policeman slowly drove his car up a trail-like road that led to the front of the medicine man's house. Rolling down the window on the driver's side and placing his left elbow out the window, he sat there waiting and looking around as his car engine continued to idle. He saw no one. After a few minutes he turned the engine off and waited some more. Everything was quiet. Not even a breeze stirred, which was extremely unusual out on the prairie. A half-grown dog came around the corner of the house but didn't bark and didn't even seem to notice the policeman and his car. It just lay down near the end of the old weatherworn porch. The whole world seemed to be engulfed in stillness.

The policeman opened the door and began to get out of the car. The dog looked up for only a moment, then laid its head back down between its front paws. The policeman made his way up the two steps, onto the front porch, and knocked on the edge of the screen door. He looked in the direction of the dog, who simply wagged its tail two or three times. There was no need to knock again; the door was open and he could see through the screen door that no one was in the one-room house. Then the dog got up and trotted back around the house. The policeman followed him. There stood an old man near the top of the hill, facing each of the four directions in turn, praying. He waited for the old man near the back of the weatherbeaten old house for half an hour or longer.

Finally the old man slowly made his way down the hill, using a long stick for a cane. He was wearing dark-blue bibbed overalls, a beige long-sleeved shirt, and moccasins. The two long, thick, almost completely black braids hanging down the front of his shoulders were marks of distinction, like the creases beneath his cheekbones and across his forehead. The policeman stood speechless. Now he understood why the medicine man was called "Hanska." This man stood over seven feet tall, with an arm span that equaled his height. He was a man of impressive stature and appearance!

When he drew near, he reached out his long arm and with his long, wide hand gently grasped the policeman's hand as he said, "Ho, kola." (He spoke Lakota: "Hello, friend.") "You must be Bob White Shield, from Greenwood. I have been expecting you." "I am ready to go," he continued. "I have my things already packed." Going into the house, he picked up a bundle, rolled up and tied with three small pieces of rope. After putting his pack roll in the back seat, he and the policeman got into the front seat of the car and began the long trip to the village beside the river.

At last they came to the top of the hill overlooking Greenwood. To their left were the two cemeteries where the native people from this community had buried their dead for over a century. From this vantage point all they could see of the village were the roofs of the buildings, some of them made of old wooden shingles, others covered with tarpaper, and a few church steeples humbly pointing toward the majestic blue midwestern sky. Across the Missouri River were the rolling Nebraska hills with deep draws that had been carved out by centuries of rain and snow water. Out in the middle of the river they could see four boats slowly making their way back and forth, still dragging. On the bank was a crowd of people, some of them huddled in small groups while others milled around with an air of impatience.

Some of them began drifting toward the church yard; it was apparent that they had seen the BIA police car. At the bottom of the hill the car turned west for a short distance, then followed the driveway around the back of the Episcopal church and parked under a tree that stood to the east of the parish house. About forty people gathered near the car, some coming from inside the parish house and others from down by the river. Among them were five members of the boy's family. After being introduced to them, the medicine man expressed his sympathy and offered words of sustaining strength and comfort.

It was now near five o'clock in the afternoon. The old man looked up into the sky and all around and said, "It is too light to work. We will have to wait until the sun goes down; then we can do our work."

He was led into the parish hall, where a meal was set for him and the family, along with some of the older members of the crowd. After he finished eating, the old man made his way among the people, shaking hands and visiting with them. He evidenced a great charisma as he gracefully made his way from person to person, visiting with both young and old, speaking English and Lakota with great eloquence.

Turning toward the whole crowd of people, who were visiting with one another, he commanded silence and respect by his stature and his very presence. He began to speak: "It is now time to work. In a few minutes I will put up my tent, where I will build a fire and heat some rocks for my sweat. We must purify ourselves before we pray to Wankantanka (the Great Spirit). When I come out of the tent, I will have just my blanket covering my body. I have no shame about me. Continue to pray to Wankantanka while I have my sweat."

He immediately put up his tent in the church yard and built a fire around a few medium-sized rocks. When it was time, he went into the tent with a pail of water and closed the tent flap behind him. The people could hear him pouring water over the hot rocks as he sang and prayed to Wankantanka. After a while he came out of the tent covered with his blanket and continuing to sing. In the meantime the earth had darkened but twilight lingered in the sky. As he sang he looked up into the sky, facing the four directions in turn. Suddenly the sky directly overhead was filled with owls circling around him. He walked down to the river, followed by the crowd and the circling owls. He stood at the edge of the water singing and talking to the river. Turning to the crowd, he said, "I am going to walk downstream. I want everyone to stay here; do not follow me."

As he walked along the shore, flashing streams of light came up from the water, like sharp flashes of lightning. When he returned, he said to the family and the rest of the crowd, "Where you saw the flashing lights come out of the water, that is where his body went. Do not bother to continue your search any longer tonight. You will not find him." Looking directly at the family, he said, "Your son's body will be found early tomorrow morning, down there, around the bend, on the other side of the river. The person who finds him will be someone who has never looked for him and will not be looking for him when he finds him. The left shoulder of his shirt will be torn. Hecetu." ("So it is.") And he walked back up toward the parish house with a quiet confidence because he knew Who was in control of the universe.

Early the next morning an old white fisherman checking his traps on the Nebraska side of the river found the young boy's body floating near the shore. The left shoulder of the boy's shirt was torn.

This was an event that happened in my lifetime, but Grandma told and retold the story, sometimes with amazing accuracy and detail, other times in a capsule form. Whichever way she chose to tell it, she made it come alive and filled it with anticipation and mystery until I could feel my heartbeat quicken.

Night after night she told story after story. I suppose when I wasn't there she thought them through in her mind. She undoubtedly shared them with me because she wanted me to know and remember them, and to be able to retell them as she did. Perhaps even more, she told them in order to keep in touch with her beginnings, those beginnings that reappeared every time she wandered through the pages of her early life, as though they had happened early that morning. They were very much a part of who she was, where she came from. And as she put life into each and every story, each and every story put life into her.

17

Some events and experiences make an impact upon our lives far beyond our imagination and awareness. They come into our lives at some of the most unexpected times, like the sliding of a prayer book in front of me one Sunday morning. Images are here in our minds, images like that of an old woman kneeling beside her bed or at an altar, praying.

Owls come sweeping into the deep places of our lives, if only momentarily, and call our name or the name of someone we love more than we love ourselves, and it influences the way we think and how we feel.

Other creatures are here and there, now and then, not with any particular stern message, but to add beauty and meaning to life. The cunning crow always seems to call to remind us that we're never alone. The meadowlark year after year makes us aware that we all have a common song of life to sing. The mischievous bluejays with their strident cries sometimes force us from the level of laughter to a place of pain and suffering, where we discover and rediscover what we believe and in Whom we believe.

Birds have always made their presence known in my life.

While walking through a meadow or a wooded area, I can hear the sound of a bird's voice above all other sounds. Even during a movie in a theater or on television, a bird chirping in the background becomes, for me, the main character of the scene.

It was another evening, so familiar that it provided security and stability for a teenager whose life was filled with indirection and uncertainty. During the past few years I had grown wings and flown away to discover what life was like beyond the nest of my childhood. Living with Mom for a while in Sioux City during the seventh grade turned out to be an unhappy experience. A few months with Dad in Rapid City, South Dakota, was more stressful and divisive than I could understand. Always, as if attached by an umbilical cord, I retraced my steps back to that little brown house on Choteau Creek for spiritual and emotional nourishment. It was a nesting place and a resting place built upon solid values and basic beliefs that I could depend on.

Tonight Grandma sat in her usual position. She was now nearly eighty years old, with eyesight that imposed more and more limitations upon her. She was unable to do some of the things she loved to do: her Bible had been put away some time before, she no longer cooked from new recipes, sewing was now something of her past, and she constantly shaded her eyes with her hand in an attempt to identify clouded objects. Perhaps her limited eyesight is what caused her to withdraw. Since she could not see well on the outside, gazing on the inside and reflecting on what she could see was a compensation for her.

There she was, feet crossed, forehead in the palm of her right hand, eyes closed. "Grandma," I said in a very diffident manner, "there is an image that I keep remembering, and I don't know where I saw it." Before I could go on, she asked, "What is it? What kind of image is it?" "It's an image of a bird," I answered. "It is yellow and is in a cage."

Grandma looked in my direction for a moment. It was like an invitation to go on a journey back in time with her. She closed her eyes and partially covered them again. She rubbed her fingers on her forehead a few times by nodding her head up and down. "When you were about a year and a half old," she began, "you became terribly ill. We thought we were going to lose you. You were growing and doing so well. You were walking, talking, and feeding yourself." She paused for a few moments before she continued, "Then you got sick. Your dad and mother took you to the hospital. I went with them. After the doctor examined you, they brought you out into the waiting room, where I was sitting. While they were in talking with the doctor, I held you in my arms."

Grandma dropped her chin until it nearly rested on her chest. Repositioning her hand on her forehead to cover her eyes, she continued, "Your lips were so dry and cracked, your face was so pale, that I thought you were close to dying. Over in the corner there was this stand that had a bird cage sitting on it. In the cage there was a yellow canary."

Putting her first two fingers on her lips and looking toward me, she said, "When you heard that bird singing, you opened your eyes and tried to smile, but you couldn't; your lips were too dry and you were too weak. So you went back to sleep." Resuming her original position, she paused for what seemed a long while, then quietly added, "That must be the bird you remember."

Grandma had my attention. She may have been ready to return to the present, but I wasn't. Moving to the very edge of my chair and resting my arms on the kitchen table, I urged her on, wanting to know more. "What happened?"

"Well, they took you back into the hospital," Grandma explained, "and the doctor stayed up all night with you. At first he didn't think you would make it through the night. But he saw you through."

Without moving the rest of her body, Grandma sat up straight. She continued, "Your dad went home, back to Greenwood, and asked the people from the Presbyterian church to have a prayer meeting for you. Several people came and gathered in the church just to pray for your healing. One elder by the name of Albert Jandreau asked God to heal you and lead you into Christian service."

Moving her hand from her forehead and crossing her arms in front of her, she stared down at the floor and said, "When you got well, you had to learn to walk, and talk, and feed yourself all over again. But we have always been thankful that God answered Albert Jandreau's prayer and you're still alive."

Grandma didn't say another word the rest of the night. She simply sat there with her eyes closed. I couldn't help but wonder where she was and what kind of thoughts were going through her mind. I knew, however, what was going through my mind. After hearing Grandma tell that story, I began to understand some things about myself. For the first time I began to recognize the force behind my desire to be a minister. In fact, that night I realized that there had never been a time in my life when I didn't want to be a minister, at least as far as I could remember. That night I also understood why Grandma would have me read the prayers on Sunday morning without first asking me. It was like pieces of a puzzle coming together that night. Other pieces came together in the nights ahead.

Another piece of the puzzle fell into place as Grandma sat in her usual storytelling posture. This night she chose to dramatize stories from the Bible. It was amazing how she could make all those people and events come alive while simply sitting there with her eyes closed and her hand over her forehead. Her language, diction, and tone of her voice made those characters as real and personal as her father and mother and other people from her past. She made me experience their pain and share their joy. I was caught up in the mystery and miracles of their own time.

Before I realized it, Grandma was looking in my direction and telling me what it meant to be a Christian. She promised nothing easy, only meaningful. She never said it would be without pain, but that there would be an inner peace. She didn't even say that everyone would like me, but that there is One who loves me and would always be with me. That night Grandma said, "Being a Christian means believing in God, in Christ, in others, and in yourself." She went on, "There comes a time, my boy, when everyone must accept, for themselves, the responsibility of their relationship with God through Christ. And for someone to say nothing is for someone to say 'No.'" She looked back toward the floor and waited. There was a complete silence.

It was, unexpectedly, my move. It was my choice, to give a silent "No" or an audible "Yes." We sat in silence for only a few seconds, but it seemed like hours. I felt as if the whole world was watching and waiting for an answer from me. There was something very final about this decision. A panorama of my life passed before me, and I could see how this event and that experience, led and influenced by Grandma and others, had brought me to this place of no return.

"Grandma," I asked, "how do I accept this responsibility for myself? What do I have to do?" "Just kneel down and tell God what you want to do," she answered. She looked in my direction again.

This was a serious matter, one that touched the very heart of our lives. The moistness around Grandma's eyes was an indication of how personal and urgent this was to her.

"I will help you," she said. "Come," she continued, "I will kneel with you and pray with you." We knelt together on the rough and dusty kitchen floor, she on one side of her chair and I on the other side. Grandma held my hands in her long, thin hands. This time she didn't cover her face, preferring to hold my hands. Still, the expression on her face was a clear indication that she was going off into another world as she conversed with her Creator. What was so awesome about this prayer, and different from her other prayer journeys, was that this time she was taking me with her! Perhaps that is why she held my hand. Kneeling on the floor I had swept and mopped so many times, and in a room where I had heard so many stories from Grandma, I learned the meaning of the Biblical term "mountain-top" experience.

Because Grandma had set the tone and had shown me the way, not just tonight but many times before, I was able to do what I needed to do that night. I prayed a prayer like I had never prayed before or since. I somehow gained enough courage to tell God all about me. It was like I had been freed from my past and given a fresh, new start.

It must have been a gratifying experience for Grandma, too. To think that her grandson, whom she loved so deeply, had stepped into that other world with her brought tears to her eyes. When we stood up, she hugged me and cried, not as she had at the cemetery, nor the day she saw her son standing before her, but like she did the day David came home. It must have been like another home-coming for her.

The test of my faith in God came during my high school days. After I completed the eighth grade in the one-room schoolhouse, Grandma and Grandpa encouraged me to continue my educa-tion, even if it meant leaving home to do so. In the fall of 1954 I went to Kansas City to live with Mom during the ninth grade, another stressful experience. David was there, and married by now. There were times when if it hadn't been for him, I don't know what I would have done. As soon as the school year ended, I returned to that old house, and to Grandpa and Grandma.

I could see that getting my education was not going to be an easy task. Grandma and Grandpa were both failing in health and needed someone to check on them more frequently. In addition, there would be such obstacles as finances, housing, and transportation. Going to high school meant moving eighteen miles away to Wagner, where the nearest high school in Charles Mix County was. It meant being away all week and hitchhiking or walking home on weekends.

Grandma found a place where I could stay during the week. She talked with a woman who claimed Grandma as her cousin. This woman consented to let me stay with her and her family at a very reasonable charge. Eventually she claimed me as her grandson, and she continued to be another grandmother to me until she died.

For a time everything went well, living with this family during the week, although when Friday came, part of me dreaded the long journey back home, then back to town again on Sunday afternoon. At the same time another part of me, an even more important part of me, looked forward to going home and being with those two old people. Every weekend, however, it became apparent that they were failing in so many little ways that it was difficult to leave them home. Yet every Sunday afternoon they encouraged me to go back to school and assured me that they would be all right, since I had replenished their water supply and sometimes their groceries.

I wondered how we were going to manage this whole affair during the winter months. They would need fuel every day, and someone to help them keep the fires burning. I also knew there would be some weekends when I would not be able to come home because of the cold and snow. It was a concern of mine, but they continued to tell me that it would all work out.

Finances eventually became a burden. As time went by, my room and board added up to a sizable amount. In that small community there were very few after-school jobs available, and even fewer for Indians. In an effort to get some help I tried to find Dad, but could not locate him. The next thing was to get in touch with Mom to ask for some kind of support, but that proved fruitless. The week before Thanksgiving I stopped by the high school superintendent's office to tell him I was considering dropping out of school. Almost immediately he called the social worker and attempted to get some financial assistance for me. He concluded unhappily, though, that would involve too much white tape. The week of Thanksgiving 1955, I quit school and went back to that little brown house on Choteau Creek.

In some ways it was a relief to be back home, although I still had a debt that needed to be paid someday. At least it wasn't accumulating now. In addition, I knew someone was there to provide the care and help that Grandma and Grandpa needed. But I returned home with negative feelings. I was disappointed because I couldn't continue my education. Even more, I was angry and bitter. Grandma sensed the latter without my even verbalizing it. One evening while we were washing dishes, she said, "Always remember, my boy, a person can never control bitterness. Bitterness always control the person." Nothing more was said about the subject, that night or any other time afterward.

Several nights later Grandma and I found ourselves in the same familiar setting. She was sitting in her usual place, in her comfortable, thoughtful position, with the kitchen table and the kerosene lamp between us. I began to lash out. "Grandma, nobody seems to care. Mom doesn't care. Dad doesn't care. The social worker doesn't care. The superintendent doesn't care. No body seems to care." I began to cry.

Through my tear-filled eyes I could see Grandma sitting there with her eyes closed as though she was trying to give me the privacy that I needed in which to cry. When my tears and sighs subsided, she looked in my direction and asked, "My boy, you believe in God, don't you?" "Yes," I responded. I waited for her to say more, but she didn't. She simply closed her eyes and covered her forehead with her hand. Perhaps she didn't say any more because there was nothing more to say.

That night I realized I was back in that house not just because Grandpa and Grandma needed me to help them, but because I needed them. During a time when I so desperately needed to know that I had someone who cared for me, they were there, loving and caring as they always did. They were that sustaining force when I needed it.

For a teenager who sometimes longed to try his wings, some of the days and nights seemed endless. There was not much to do to occupy my time but to listen to the radio, fish, and do the necessary chores. We had no books or magazines to read, and anyway the lamplight was too dim to read by for any length of time. So night after night, Grandma and I entertained each other by visiting and telling funny stories. And her old and familiar stories continued to be as fresh as they were the first time I heard them.

Every night I blew out the lamp, although it didn't have the meaning that it once had for me. The shadows from the fire still danced and jumped on the ceiling. I found comfort and security in this place, even though I knew our life here could not go on forever. Someday there would be no brown house to which I could return when I felt the need. For now, however, the shadows were dancing, I would soon be overcome by sleep, and tomorrow would be another day.

18

It is amazing how quickly those endless days and nights passed. As the Psalmist wrote centuries ago, "A thousand years . . . are but as yesterday when it is past." It must be a law of life: everything seems short and swift after it is over. Sometimes we wish we could turn the clock back and do it over, but being the persons that we are, we probably wouldn't do things much differently. The outcome would be very much the same, and time would pass by equally as fast.

What is sometimes more difficult to face and accept than the passage of time is evidences that lead to endings. Resist and struggle as we might, there are times when we are forced to let something go.

The long days and nights of late winter and early spring were past, and now we were forced to think about what we would do this summer and how we would manage in the fall. The cleaning and cultivating of the garden was something that now happened only in memory, and occasionally in Grandpa's conversation. Fishing was the pastime that he talked about most and planned to do again, but never did. Bringing a fresh cup of coffee to share with Grandma in bed didn't happen any more. As the hot summer months dragged on, Grandpa became more difficult to please when he wasn't sleeping. In their day-to-day relationship Grandpa became abusive to Grandma, yet always wanted her near and was very much dependent upon her. When questions were posed about their livelihood and welfare, he would respond, "Your Grandma can do it. She will take care of that. Don't worry."

Often there were misunderstandings, and it was not always certain where he was coming from and what he wanted, but there was one concern which he very clearly voiced, again and again: "I don't want to have to live without your Grandma." Why this was a major worry of his I never knew. Perhaps, being aware that Grandma was five years older than he, maybe Grandpa was afraid she would die before him. That, for him, would have been the ultimate unbearable loss.

In her more rational periods, Grandma still displayed a kind of quiet, steady wisdom. She knew there would have to be some changes, and soon. She accepted the fact that she not only had no food to can; she didn't have the eyesight or the physical energy to can food as she once had. She was also aware that she didn't have the strength to haul water as Grandpa said she could.

The house was owned by Art Satler, and was in his pasture. They had grown accustomed to his cattle being around and sometimes coming near the house. This summer, from time to time, Grandma began referring to the grazing cows as buffalo. Once she remarked, "I saw my father standing out there, watching the buffalo." When she said this it caused Grandpa's eyes to get big, his face to turn pale, and his lips to quiver. He was being confronted with that which he had worked so hard to ignore and deny. But neither did he attempt to deny the reality of an experience that was so precious to her. He just sat there looking at her, listening to her, and sniffing a time or two.

It was becoming more and more apparent that both Grandma's and Grandpa's health was failing, physically and mentally. There were times when they recognized it, and other times when they denied it.

What was true about their health was also true about the condition of the house. It too was deteriorating rapidly. The porch by now had rotted away, the roof leaked in too many places to count, and the doors no longer closed tight enough to keep out bugs and other intruders. Yet Grandpa continued to hold fast to his stance: "There is nothing wrong with this old house. We have lived here over thirty years, and we're not going to move to town."

One morning, however, the degenerated condition of the old house was forced upon them when Grandma found a snake in the old kitchen. Even for me, that little brown house had become a place that was located in the middle of nowhere.

Planting and harvest seasons quickly swept through our lives that year, but not before I could earn money to buy some new clothes and an old car. I was up early in the mornings and out in the fields with the farmers, or sometimes by myself, working from dawn to dusk. After a few paychecks I managed to buy an old automobile, a 1938 Chevy coupe. Its faded green paint was worn clear through in spots, the seats were torn, with cotton and springs sticking out, and the floorboards were such that through them one could see the ground. It was nothing to brag about, and not much to look at, but I hoped it would provide dependable transportation throughout the summer and into the fall when I would go back to school. The one thing that old car did was to provide an opportunity to work for farmers who lived farther away. In some instances I was able to come home in the evenings to help Grandpa and Grandma.

One week, however, I was working too far away and too late in the evenings to drive back and forth every day. I left on Monday morning knowing I wouldn't be back until late Friday or Saturday. When I left, Grandpa and Grandma were getting low on groceries, but that didn't matter, since it was near the first of the month and their checks were in. Their old-age pension checks were always sent to the store where they did their trading. It was safer that way, since their mailbox was about two miles from the house, in front of the schoolhouse. The checks always arrived on the second or third of the month. While I was gone, this week, someone was going to take them to town to pay their bill from the previous month and charge enough groceries to last through the coming month. I knew that by the time I came home at the end of the week, their stock of groceries would be replenished.

When I arrived home on Friday evening, however, I found them without any food in the house. They had gone to town on Tuesday, as planned, but Grandpa and the store owner had had a misunderstanding, and Grandpa had lost his temper. As a result, the storekeeper refused to allow them to charge any more groceries, and neither would he give them their checks until he talked with the social worker. They were both upset; Grandpa was still angry and Grandma was brokenhearted. Grandma said, "I don't have anything to feed you because we ate our last bit of food today at noon." I assured her that I would be okay and wouldn't starve.

The next morning Grandma and I drove back to town. When I tried to learn his side of the story, I found the storekeeper was still angry. He was adamant that he would not do business with Grandpa and Grandma until he saw the social worker, which would not happen until Monday morning. I said to him, "Since you did not have any disagreement with Grandma, and since she didn't have any part of this, will you let her have her check, and do business with her?" "No!" he replied emphatically. "They can come back on Monday afternoon, after I have seen the social worker. We'll decide what to do then."

Grandma began to cry. "She is crying," I said, "because she

169

feels bad about this, and because they have no food to eat." I could feel my face getting hot and my hands began to tremble. "You have their checks," I shouted, "because it was a matter of convenience for you and them, not because you are their guardian. You have no right to keep their checks while they have no food to eat." He turned pale.

Touching me on my arm, Grandma gently said, "Come, my boy, we have said enough. We will come back on Monday." At that we left. We went down the street to the other store, where I bought enough groceries to last the weekend and into the coming week.

When we arrived home, Grandpa wanted to know how things went. I answered, "We got some groceries, and we're to go back on Monday afternoon." That was all that was said.

On Monday I took them back to the store. They were given their checks, and they paid their bill. But the storekeeper allowed only Grandma to charge groceries there from that time on. This meant they had to live on half their usual amount of groceries for that month. But we managed, and as always, we made it through.

In spite of her poor eyesight, Grandma seemed to know and understand "more than meets the eye." Although Grandpa and I didn't know it at the time, Grandma did not allow her hens to set that summer. Every time they tried, she found their nests and took their eggs away. All through the summer as people came to visit or to buy eggs or chickens, she gave more and more chickens away. By the end of the summer she had only a few left, mostly those that were given names. Giving her chickens away this time was very painful for her. It meant letting go of an important part of her life.

At the beginning of fall, when it was time to start school again, my faithful old car began to be undependable. Knowing that it would cost too much to fix it, I managed to sell it for a little bit of money. That was better than nothing. Before I gave it up, I moved most of my clothes back to my "other grandma's" house and started school. Fortunately, the weather continued to be nice and I hitchhiked back home every weekend. One Friday, because I managed to catch some good rides, I arrived home early. As I approached the house, there seemed to be no life outside the house. It puzzled me. I walked into the house and greeted Grandpa and Grandma. Passing by the east window in the middle room, I glanced out, and was surprised to see that the chicken coop was gone. "What happened to the chicken coop?" I immediately asked Grandma. She said, "I gave it back to Dan Jandreau. I gave them the rest of the chickens, too."

Before we could say any more, Grandpa called me. I went to his bed and sat on the edge of it, beside him. "Did your Grandma tell you the news?" he asked. "No." I answered. "We have decided to move to town," he said, "and the social worker is going to find us a place to rent." He paused for a moment, then went on, "No, we can't live in this house another winter. We'd never make it."

Not much more was said that night. For sentimental reasons I was not eager for them to move, but for me, a worry was being relieved. Several weeks later in that fall of 1956 they took what few belonging they had and moved to another small three-room house, in Wagner. When all their furniture was on the truck, both Grandma and Grandpa went back into the house, hand in hand, like a bride and groom looking at their first house. They walked from room to room talking to each one, saying good-bye and thanking them for providing shelter "all these years." Grandma looked around as though she could see perfectly clearly. Covering her eyes with her left hand, she began to cry. Grandpa just stood there, body stooped forward, his cane in his right hand and Grandma's hand in his left, letting the tears run down his face and drip off his chin. Together they slowly made their way through the old kitchen and outside. While Grandma got into the back seat of the car that I had borrowed, Grandpa wired the front door to the house shut.

The truck had gone on ahead of us. Stopping to close behind us the gate that kept the cattle in the pasture, Grandma and Grandpa looked back with saddened faces and heavy hearts. They were leaving behind not only a place but a large and important part of their lives together. It was the last time they saw that little brown house on Choteau Creek.

A few weeks after they were moved in and settled, I bought Grandma and Grandpa a used washing machine and a refrigerator with the money I had been saving. For the first time in their lives they had electricity. "Now," I said, "you can have electric appliances." They were well pleased with my purchase.

In addition, I decided to buy some new clothes for them, and such things as towels and wash cloths. I intended to buy Grandpa a new pair of overalls, and two new dresses for Grandma. I knew Grandma's size, but not Grandpa's. So I told him what I was going to do and asked, "Grandpa, what size overalls do you wear?" "A size forty-four." he said. I thought to myself, "That couldn't be. Maybe he used to wear that size, but not now. I'll buy a size thirty-six for him and hope he doesn't ask about the size." That is what I did.

But, when I showed Grandpa the new overalls, the first thing he asked was, "What size are they?" I had to tell him the truth. He sat up and said, "They'll never fit. They're too small." Even so, I asked him to try them on. I helped him take off his old pair and slip on the new ones. To my relief and his surprise, they fit him almost perfectly. Looking at me and smiling, he said, "I must be getting pretty small." He thanked me and lay back down.

We shared a happy year in the house on the edge of town. Grandpa and Grandma probably ate more fresh meat and fruit, more ice cream and Jello than they had ever eaten before in their lives. The house was much warmer and easier to keep clean than the one they had left. Knowing the grief they were both experiencing as a result of the move, I tried to make life as comfortable as possible for them.

Grandma unexpectedly announced one day that she was going to the eye doctor to see if anything could be done to improve her vision. A week or so later she did go to the hospital, which was now only six blocks away, to get her eyes examined. When she returned she told us that they wanted her to go to Omaha for eye surgery. With fear written all over his face, Grandpa said, "You told them you couldn't go, didn't you?" Grandma's face fell in disappointment. She wanted to go. She replied, "I told them I would go." Grandpa didn't speak. Grandma went on, "They will take me down there and bring me back. The doctor said I'll be gone for about a week."

"Grandpa," I assured him, "I'll be here with you, and she'll be all right." But he never said a word. The following week Grandma was taken to Omaha early on a Monday morning. Though he never mentioned it, Grandpa missed her tremendously.

The next afternoon, a car drove up with several people in it. The back door opened and Grandma got out. She closed the door and the vehicle was gone. I was surprised that she was back so soon. I greeted her as she entered the house and went in to kiss Grandpa. "What happened?" he immediately asked. "How come you're back so soon?" "Because there is nothing that can be done about my eyes." She continued, "The doctor said they're too far gone." There was disappointment in her voice and sadness in her eyes, but it was clear that she had accepted her situation and was prepared to live with it the rest of her life.

For some time I had been experiencing growing pains. I had dreamed for years about joining the air force. It just seemed like now was the time to go. I called Mom, who was now living and working in Omaha, and talked with her about it. I said, "Mom, I have taken care of Grandma and Grandpa all these years. Now, I think, it is time that you come home and take care of them for the rest of their lives." To my surprise, she agreed.

I enlisted in the air force in July 1957, and was called to go in early September. When I announced the plan to Grandpa and Grandma they both just sat very still, staring at the floor. Then Grandma looked at me and said, "Your mother said she is coming?" "Yes," I replied. "My, that will be nice," she observed.

The time to leave came sooner than I realized. Before I knew it, my clothes were packed and the recruiter's car was parked in front of the house. It was time to go, and I wasn't sure if I was ready to leave two of the dearest people in the whole world.

Walking into the bedroom where Grandpa was lying, I put on a brave front. "Well, Grandpa," I said, "it's time for me to go." Before I could say more, he sat up and said, "My boy, you take good care of yourself, and be good, and we'll remember you in our prayers." He sat there with his hands resting on the edge of the bed, beside him. Looking down at the floor, he began to cry.

As I stood there watching him cry, a distant memory came vividly to my mind. It was when I was a little boy, and Grandma had become very sick. I remembered her making her way about the house, from one piece of furniture to another, slowly and in great pain. A neighbor came with his car to take Grandma to the hospital. Because she was too sick even to walk out to the car, she sat in a straight-backed chair while the neighbor and Grandpa carried her to the car. When they picked her up, it frightened her, and when she got scared, I got scared and began to cry. After they settled her in the back seat of the car, Grandpa turned to me and, with his big red handkerchief, dried my tears and wiped my nose. He did it many times after that, but that was the very first time I could remember.

And there I stood, now a young man, watching an old man

whom I loved so deeply cry. He didn't even try to hide his emotions or dry his tears. Taking my handkerchief out of my pocket, I put one hand on his back and with the other wiped away his tears. The last thing I did for this wonderful man, who had so many times in the past dried my tears, was to dry his tears. It was a humbling privilege and honor.

Grandma was waiting for me out on the porch. When I walked out the door, she hugged me and began to cry. After she regained her composure, she pulled my face close so she could see me, and said, "My boy, you have always been like our own, since the time you were very young. We will miss you, but you are a man now and you must go. God will take care of you."

She patted both my shoulders at the same time, very gently, but leaving a touch that will last forever. I turned and slowly walked to the recruiter's car. I got in the front seat with him and we backed out of the yard, leaving Grandma standing on the front porch, watching. With her hand shading her eyes, she was watching another ending of something very important in her life. The recruiter stopped at the stop sign. Looking back, I could see her still standing there. She looked like she could see forever, and maybe she could.

We turned the corner and I couldn't see her any more.

This was the ending I had dreaded so much. But if I could turn the clock back and do it over, there wouldn't be very much that I would want to change. Grandpa and Grandma gave to me what I needed most, someone to guide and care for me. And I gave to them, perhaps, what they needed most, a son and someone to love. I wouldn't want to change that for anything in the world.

Epilogue

Mom moved back with Grandpa and Grandma a few days after I left and cared for them for the rest of their lives. Grandpa died ten months after I drove away with the air force recruiter. I went home to see him when he was critically ill, but he was not aware of much during my visit. It consisted mostly of my sitting in the hospital room with him, hour after hour. The last time I saw and spoke to him was about two o'clock in the morning of the day I left. I looked up and saw him clawing at the oxygen tent to get my attention. After I got under the tent so we could talk, he asked me what I was doing there in his room. I explained that I had been with him for the past ten days but that I was leaving in the morning and would not be back for a long time. His last words to me were, "My boy, don't worry about me. I have been prepared for this a long time." He died on June 30 (Grandma's birthday), 1958. He was seventy-six years old.

Grandma lived nearly three years longer. As the years passed, she became very frail and weak. She died on March 12, 1961, in her sleep. The physician said she died of old age; all her organs just wore out. She was eighty-three years old. Both Grandpa and

Grandma were buried beside their son on that hill overlooking the Missouri River.

Mom got a job at the Indian Health Hospital and worked there until she was forced to go on disability because of a crippling arthritis. She had overcome her drinking problem and become an exceptionally supportive mother. She died in November 1983, about a year and a half after Phillip, and is buried beside him in the cemetery just south of Egan, South Dakota. She was seventy-two years old.

Phillip had come home about a year after he was wounded, but was confined to a wheelchair for several years. After a number of stays in the V.A. hospital and some physical therapy, he improved to the point that he could walk using only a cane. He married a young woman from home and raised a large family. He died suddenly in June 1982, when he was forty-nine years old. He was one of the best brothers I could have had.

Dorothy left that Christmas of 1948 and never returned to live there again. She got married at an early age and raised a family, not without personal struggles. Occasionally she would go back to that little house to visit, but not for very long. All of her children are now adults and keep close contact with her. She currently lives in Minnesota.

David left home before he finished the eighth grade but he maintained a close relationship with Grandpa and Grandma. He got married, raised a family, and lives in South Dakota, about one hundred miles from that old place. Looking back, he feels "Ever since Grandpa and Grandma died, I haven't had a home."

Dad moved here and there for most of his life. While he was doing this, he was married and divorced several times. He never made being a father a high priority in his life, and as his children grew older, they all sort of let him go and drifted away from him. He eventually returned to the reservation, when he was of retirement age, and lived there until he died. During his last days I had the privilege and burden of caring for him as he suffered from bone cancer. He died in September 1987 and is buried in the cemetery on the hill overlooking the village of Greenwood and the Missouri River, about ten miles west of Grandpa and Grandma's burial place. He was seventy-four years old.

As for me, I stayed in the air force for eight years. During that time I was married and had four children. After I was discharged I got a college education, seminary training, and became a United Methodist minister. I have served churches in Florida, Michigan, and South Dakota. Currently I am a doctoral student in the Department of Child Development and Family Relations at the University of North Carolina at Greensboro. Now and then I go back to that old house to find myself; it's so easy to get lost in the world. I return there to rediscover my roots—who I am, where I came from—and to recall some of the basic fundamental principles of life, like love, faith in God, and giving.